W9-DHY-302

101 KEY IDEAS

PHILOSOPHY

THIS IS NONSENSE. THIS IS
UTTERLY NONSENSE.

CRITIQUE

101 KEY IDEAS

PHILOSOPHY

Paul Oliver

TEACH YOURSELF BOOKS

For UK orders: please contact Bookpoint Ltd, 130 Milton Park, Abingdon, Oxon OX14 4SB. Telephone: (44) 01235 827720, Fax: (44) 01235 400454. Lines are open from 09.00–18.00, Monday to Saturday, with a 24-hour message answering service. Email address: orders@bookpoint.co.uk

For U.S.A. order enquiries: please contact McGraw-Hill Customer Services, P.O. Box 545, Blacklick, OH 43004-0545, U.S.A. Telephone 1-800-722-4726. Fax: 1-614-755-5645.

For Canada order enquiries: please contact McGraw-Hill Ryerson Ltd., 300 Water St, Whitby, Ontario L1N 9B6, Canada. Telephone: 905 430 5000. Fax: 905 430 5020.

Long renowned as the authoritative source for self-guided learning – with more than 30 million copies sold worldwide – the *Teach Yourself* series includes over 300 titles in the fields of languages, crafts, hobbies, business and education.

British Library Cataloguing in Publication Data
A catalogue record for this title is available from The British Library

Library of Congress Catalog Card Number: On file

First published in UK 2000 by Hodder Headline Plc, 338 Euston Road, London NW1 3BH.

First published in US 2000 by Contemporary Books, A Division of The McGraw-Hill Companies, 4255 West Touhy Avenue, Lincolnwood (Chicago), Illinois 60712-1975 U.S.A.

The 'Teach Yourself' name and logo are registered trade marks of Hodder & Stoughton Ltd.

Copyright © 2000 Paul Oliver

Cover design and illustration by Mike Stones

Typeset by Transet Limited, Coventry, England
Printed in Great Britain for Hodder & Stoughton Educational, a division of Hodder Headline Ltd, 338 Euston Road, London NW1 3BH by Cox & Wyman Ltd, Reading, Berkshire.

Impression number   10 9 8 7 6 5 4 3
Year   2007 2006 2005 2004 2003 2002 2001

Contents

Introduction

Welcome to the **Teach Yourself 101 Key Ideas** series. We hope that you will find both this book and others in the series to be useful, interesting and informative. The purpose of the series is to provide an introduction to a wide range of subjects, in a way that is entertaining and easy to absorb.

Each book contains 101 short accounts of key ideas or terms which are regarded as central to that subject. The accounts are presented in alphabetical order for ease of reference. All of the books in the series are written in order to be meaningful whether or not you have previous knowledge of the subject. They will be useful to you whether you are a general reader, are on a pre-university course, or have just started at university.

We have designed the series to be a combination of a text book and a dictionary. We felt that many text books are too long for easy reference, while the entries in dictionaries are often too short to provide sufficient detail. The **Teach Yourself 101 Key Ideas** series gives the best of both worlds! Here are books that you do not have to read cover to cover, or in any set order. Dip into them when you need to know the meaning of a term, and you will find a short, but comprehensive account which will be of real help with those essays and assignments. The terms are described in a straightforward way with a careful selection of academic words thrown in for good measure!

So if you need a quick and inexpensive introduction to a subject, **Teach Yourself 101 Key Ideas** is for you. And incidentally, if you have any suggestions about this book or the series, do let us know. It would be great to hear from you.

Best wishes with your studies!

Paul Oliver
Series Editor

A Priori

Epistemology is the branch of philosophy concerned with the study of knowledge as a subject in its own right. In particular, epistemology involves examining the grounds on which we claim to know that something is true or false. In this sense *a priori* knowledge is described as knowledge which is not based on observations of the world around us. The latter kind of knowledge is often termed empirical knowledge, or perhaps less commonly, *a posteriori* knowledge.

Common sense suggests that most of our knowledge comes from either observations of the world, or perhaps from our senses of touch and hearing. If we observe a chair which has been painted blue, we know it is a blue chair because of our interpretation of a particular wavelength of light received by our eyes. In addition, we understand the concept 'blue' because as we grew up we learned that objects with this colour were described as blue. If on the other hand someone says to us that there is a chair in the next room, we have no way of knowing in advance what colour the chair might be. There is nothing in the concept 'chair' which helps us to predict its colour.

Now some philosophers argue that all knowledge must of necessity be based upon empirical observation. Such philosophers can generally be described as empiricists. Others suggest, however, that *a priori* knowledge, i.e. derived prior to experience, is perfectly possible. Philosophers who hold this position can be broadly described as rationalists. As an example of knowledge which some might argue is *a priori*, we could take the idea that every event in the universe must have a cause. An advocate of the existence of *a priori* knowledge would say that if we were told a ball had been seen rolling down the road, we would know that something had caused the ball to start rolling. It might have been a gust of wind, or someone kicking it, or that the road was sloping. A rationalist would argue that there would be no need to investigate the ball-rolling incident any further in order to determine that something had caused the event.

see also...
Analytic Proposition; Empiricism

Absolutism

This is the general philosophical view that there are fundamental truths about the world which are independent of the opinions of individual people or of different societies. It is a term which is often used in the area of ethics and, to some extent, in that of politics. Ethical absolutism is the view that there are moral principles which are true in all cultures and societies, and at all times in history, irrespective of whether human beings do in fact adhere to them. Absolutism in this sense is frequently compared to ethical relativism, the view that human conduct can only be judged in relation to the specific values, circumstances and norms of either individuals or societies.

An example of an absolute moral principle could be that it is wrong to knowingly take the life of another human being. Some people might wish to extend this to the taking of life in general. If one accepts such a moral principle then one could not support capital punishment no matter how repugnant the crime committed; one could not support euthanasia no matter how great the suffering of the patient; and one could not support abortion. Moreover, if one was attacked in time of war, one would have to adopt a pacifist position and refrain from any action which might cause death to the enemy. Another example of a moral absolute could be that it is always wrong to tell a lie.

It is interesting to reflect on the possible origins of moral absolutes. They could be regarded as deriving from God, or alternatively that they are an intrinsic part of human consciousness and hence part of everyone's make-up. If, on the other hand, they are seen as having been defined by human beings, then this could be regarded as a contradiction in terms. If absolutes can be created by human beings, then presumably they can also be rejected and replaced by other absolutes.

For an absolutist, the idea of universal ethical principles is not undermined by the existence of a society in which some people do not adibe by such principles.

see also...

Relativism

Aesthetics

If you walked into an art gallery and one of the sculpture exhibits consisted of a large pile of spaghetti, would you regard this as art? Questions such as this come within the scope of aesthetics. This subject considers philosophical issues concerning the criteria by which we try to decide whether something can be defined as art. Aesthetics also explores the question of whether or not a particular artistic creation is to be regarded as 'good'. Aesthetics includes all areas of art such as painting, sculpture, literature, music and architecture, and tries to resolve philosophical questions about the purpose of art. For example, some people might argue that art should always have a practical use or contribute to society in some way. Others may suggest that the purpose of art is to allow human beings to express themselves and that no other form of justification is necessary.

Few people would probably deny that the famous sculptures of the Italian Renaissance or well-known Impressionist paintings be regarded as art. There may be differences of opinion, however, over some contemporary 'art'. It might be suggested, for example, that artistic creations should conform to certain accepted standards in terms of design, composition and execution. Establishing precise criteria to help decide whether or not something is art, remains a complex philosophical task. To some extent it is a matter of whether a work of art can be judged only in relation to other works, or whether absolute standards can be applied.

Similar difficulties arise when we attempt to specify criteria for what should count as 'good' or 'bad' art. Part of the difficulty is that fashions in art clearly change. The abstract paintings of Picasso and Braque may at one time have been misunderstood and regarded, at best, as inferior. Nowadays, of course, they are viewed differently, and are seen as a milestone in the development of twentieth-century painting. The use of public funds to support artistic endeavour has also sharpened the debate about the purposes of art.

see also...

Absolutism; Relativism

Agnosticism

An agnostic is a person who does not know whether or not a god exists. More precisely, agnostics have considered the question of the possible existence of a deity or deities and have judged that there is simply insufficient evidence either to support or negate the proposition. They do not reject the possibility of a god, but are suspending judgement for lack of evidence.

The philosophical and logical position of agnostics raises further questions about the nature of religious knowledge. If one wished to provide evidence for the existence of God, then traditionally one had recourse to either naturalistic evidence or revelatory evidence. A form of naturalistic argument would be to suggest that the structure of the world either on an atomic level, or on a cellular level in plants and animals, is so complex and wondrous, that it must have come about under the influence of a divine creator. This is a naturalistic argument because it takes as its starting point and evidence base, naturally occurring phenomena. Opponents of this type of argument would suggest that there are no logical grounds for making the connection between natural phenomena and the existence of God.

Revelatory evidence, on the other hand, suggests that knowledge of religion and God is revealed to human beings generally, or perhaps to certain selected human beings. This knowledge may then be passed on to others by the spoken word, or perhaps written down in the form of scriptures. Opponents of the concept of revelatory knowledge suggest that it is impossible to confirm the validity of the revelations; one is asked to take them on trust.

Agnostics adopt their position with regard to the existence of God, largely because they are operating within a scientific paradigm. They are applying the accepted tenets of scientific procedure to religious 'knowledge', and arguably the problem here is a mismatch between scientific knowledge and religious knowledge. There is a difference in the way criteria are applied and conclusions drawn.

see also...

Naturalism; Paradigm

Analytic Proposition

The German philosopher Immanuel Kant (1724–1804) originally made the distinction between analytic and synthetic propositions. Technically an analytic proposition is one in which the information in the predicate is already contained in the subject of the proposition. In a synthetic proposition the predicate contains additional information to that within the subject.

In the proposition 'All four-legged tables have four legs', the second half of the statement adds nothing new to our knowledge of such tables. It merely re-states the information conveyed in the subject. We cannot conceive of finding a four-legged table which does not have four legs. As therefore the predicate is contained in the subject, the proposition is analytic. Philosophers since Kant have explored the nature of analytic propositions. Such propositions are broadly understood to be those in which an analysis of the subject reveals the content of the predicate. For example, consider the proposition 'All triangles have three sides.' An analysis of the concept 'triangle' reveals that for a geometrical shape to be termed 'triangle', then it *must* have three sides. It could not have four or five sides and still legitimately be a triangle. Hence, the above proposition must be analytic.

In the propositions 'All sons have had parents' and 'All sons have had sisters', there is a distinction to be drawn between the knowledge contained in the subjects and predicates. In the first proposition it is part of the concept of being a son that one must have had biological parents. One's parents may not still be alive, but a son must have had parents at some time. Given developments in medical science, it should be possible to trace the origins of the genetic material which gave rise to conception. The first proposition is thus analytic, since it is part of the concept 'son' to have had parents. With regard to the second proposition however, it is not a necessary qualification to be a son, to have had a sister, and hence the proposition is not analytic.

see also...

Empiricism

5

Argument ad hominem

This means literally an argument directed 'to the man'. It signifies a situation where someone attempts to refute an argument by discrediting in some way the person who has made the suggestion. The attack is made against the person who has put forward the argument, rather than against the content of the argument itself. That is why the argument *ad hominem* is regarded as an example of a fallacy. An argument can only be refuted properly by assembling persuasive evidence which can be independently validated by others.

There are various ways in which the *ad hominem* argument can operate. There may be an attempt to discredit what someone is saying by asserting that the speaker is biased. Let us suppose that a local politician lives in a very pleasant country house with open views across fields and hills. This politician takes part in a debate about a housing programme to build a large, new estate in a rural location. When the politician opposes the housing development, someone says, 'Well, you would expect her to say that wouldn't you; she lives in the country herself.' Of course the issue of whether or not to build houses on a large scale in a rural situation is a complex one, but it should be decided on the evidence, rather than by trying to discredit those taking part in the discussion.

Another way in which the *ad hominem* argument may be employed is when someone tries to undermine or cast doubt on the truthfulness of a person. Someone may say, 'Well how can you accept what he is saying? Do you remember when he last spoke on this matter; it was clearly shown that he had presented only some of the evidence.' This is a fallacious argument since even if it is reasonable to criticize someone for the past, we cannot assume that what they are saying now is incorrect. Again, the correct way to refute an argument is to assemble evidence against the argument itself.

Finally, if someone tries to refute an argument by saying that the speaker is always changing his mind, then this is again an *ad hominem* argument.

see also...

Argument from Authority

Argument from Authority

In logic this is a type of fallacy in which a person tries to establish the truth of something simply by arguing that an important person or a noted authority says it is true. It can be a commonly used strategy both in everyday conversation and in serious discussion in the media. Suppose that a television interviewer is discussing economic policy with a politician, and the latter says that 'the raising of interest rates is clearly the best policy, and this was firmly established by the work of a professor last year.' This is an example of an argument from authority because the evidence presented was simply the word of the professor, rather than the research data itself. Under these circumstances the interviewer should not let the politician get away with an argument from authority, but should demand a summary of the professor's evidence, in order that the viewers can make up their own minds.

Perhaps unfortunately, many areas of life are becoming increasingly specialized with their own vocabulary and technical terms. In these circumstances it can be difficult for the layperson to decide which 'authority' to follow, even when evidence is supplied. This may be true particularly with regard to politicians who perhaps present radically opposed economic policies which are designed to achieve the same end of economic prosperity. The electorate may be provided with all kinds of historical, statistical and fiscal data, but may find it very difficult to decide between the opposing arguments. One might argue that when someone is acting as an authority, it should be possible to present evidence in a straightforward and understandable way. The key issue to remember when confronted with an argument from authority, is that it is the evidence that should matter, and not the authority.

Nevertheless, we are often quite prepared to accept a version of the argument from authority. When we visit the dentist we are usually given a brief explanation for the proposed treatment, but we do not tend to ask for all of the evidence. We accept the judgement of the dentist as an authority.

see also...

Epistemology; Truth

Asceticism

Ascetics are people who relinquish their attachments to the world as far as possible, usually because they see this as an aid to spiritual fulfilment. Hence ascetics will usually give up their homes, have limited contact with family and friends, and sustain their existence with the bare minimum of clothes and food. Some ascetics live in communities of like-minded people, while others live the life of a wandering mendicant. Ascetics may grow what limited food they need, or alternatively rely upon alms given by laypeople or disciples.

Some early Christian monastic communities may be regarded as ascetic in character. However, in terms of people living the ascetic religious life today, we must turn to the major eastern religions of Hinduism and Buddhism. In India it is relatively common to find wandering ascetics, usually referred to as *sadhus*. They may belong to a variety of Hindu sects and be devotees of different gods or goddesses. Some may live in an organized monastic community, but many others may simply wander from one holy place to another. They will typically practise

yoga, and be adept at various meditational techniques.

In Buddhism one of the central elements of religious practice is that of non-attachment. Not only is the principle applied to the non-attachment to thoughts which arise in the mind, but also to material possessions. Monks and nuns belonging to the Theravada tradition, for example, will have only a few prescribed possessions, including a robe, sandals, and bowl for receiving food alms. So strict is the non-attachment to material possessions, that they are forbidden to handle money and must rely upon lay Buddhists to provide them with the material possessions to sustain life.

In terms of broad philosophical approach, ascetics generally subscribe to the tenets of the religion to which they belong. However, they would typically share a rejection of the world of the senses as being ephemeral, illusory and of no real help in pursuing the religious life.

see also...

Cynicism

Atheism

This is the belief system that there is no God in control of the universe. Atheists generally stress the rational and materialistic explanations of the universe, rather than employing any spiritual, mystical or other-worldly explanations.

The concept of a deity or deities is certainly widespread in a variety of cultures, although this does not, of course, imply the existence of God. Atheists can draw upon a variety of psychological, sociological and historical analyses which purport to show that the notion of 'God' is a human construction rather than an objective entity. Atheists may argue that God is a product of the human mind which reflects the widespread psychological need for a controlling force in the universe, in which people can believe. Equally, it can be argued that God is a functional concept in society, in furthering social cohesion and enabling social groups to have a sense of common purpose and belonging. Within this view, God is seen as a social construction, rather than a power existing in reality. Finally, atheists may draw upon historical explanations which can suggest that God as a concept is socially powerful at stages in the historical development of societies, when there is a limited understanding of the scientific basis of the universe. They may point to the decline in the power and authority of the Church in post-medieval Europe, as the understanding of scientific principles started to spread. All of these arguments are employed by atheists to suggest that the idea of God derives from human thought and from human society and not from any independently existing entity.

Moreover atheists argue that we do not really have any need for the concept of God – there is nothing that cannot, in principle, be adequately explained by science. Even in areas where we do not yet have a full understanding, such as in the treatment of certain diseases, there is nothing to suggest that a scientific explanation will not emerge with time.

see also...

Agnosticism; Pantheism; Philosophy of Religion

Atomism

Atomism is a metaphysical system proposed in various forms by the Greeks, Democritus (about 460–361 BCE) and Epicurus (342–270 BCE). It sought to explain the functioning of the universe by means of a hypothetical system of atoms which were the essential component of both living and non-living material.

According to this system all physical material in the universe was supposed to consist of discrete particles, too small to be visible, called atoms. These atoms were of various shapes and in continuous motion. The movement of the atoms caused them to collide, and as a result of these collisions it was possible for atoms to join together in different combinations to form a variety of substances. Although objects decayed or were destroyed, the atoms of which they were composed continued to exist. The movement, collision and combination of atoms operate on the principle of cause and effect. One collision conditions an atom to move in a certain direction, and this atom in turn collides with another atom. Atoms have been in such motion for an infinite period of time. Philosophically, the important element to this metaphysical system is that there is no place in it for either Divine influence or for the intervention of mankind in the movement of atoms. The system is thus entirely determinist and outside the control of humanity. Human beings live in the world, but are subject to events rather than being capable of controlling them. Moreover, the atomic system of the Greeks sought to explain the world on a purely physical level. There was no religious or spiritual element present in their system, because deities had no control over atoms.

Such a system can tend to lead to a rather passive role in life for individuals. One can view atomism as suggesting that human beings cannot plan for the future because future events are determined solely by the pre-ordained movement of atoms. Even human thought patterns are basically atomistic in nature.

see also...

Epicureanism

Authority

We sometimes turn on the television and hear that a 'noted authority' is going to speak on an issue. We assume that the person has specialized knowledge and insights, which are perhaps lacking in someone who is not an authority. It may be worth considering, however, the process whereby someone becomes an authority. The person may have devoted many years to the study of a subject and developed a high level of scholarship. This might be the case with someone who has worked for a research organization or for a university. We might speak of someone, for example, as 'an authority on medieval, ecclesiastical manuscripts'. A person may also be considered an authority because of his or her high level of skill or extensive practical experience in a particular field, say, an aspect of gardening.

Although it is true that a person may have accumulated extensive expertise in interpreting data in a particular subject, it is perhaps important not to equate the person who is the authority, with the authoritative knowledge itself. It is arguable that a person may act as a repository for specialized knowledge, and may also transmit that knowledge, yet the same knowledge could in principle be held by other people. Of course, two different individuals who are regarded as authorities may interpret the same data in different ways. Two geologists may observe the same seismic disturbance on a measuring instrument. One may predict damage to buildings, while the other may not predict any significant consequences.

While authorities may disagree about the interpretation of data and the value judgements inherent in that process, there may be less disagreement about the data itself. Data can be checked by other specialists, both in terms of the manner in which it was collected and in terms of its apparent accuracy. Whenever we hear an authority commenting upon an issue, we almost inevitably judge the value of what is being said in terms of our assessment of that authority.

see also...

Argument from Authority

Autonomy

Generally people act autonomously if they select a course of action independently of others, based upon their own rational analysis of the options available. The application of the concept is, however, complicated by the limitations put on a person's actions by others, and also by the extent to which an individual chooses to be affected by the attempted constraints created by other people. For example, consider the case of a person working for a large organization who wishes to study part-time for a degree in sociology. He asks his manager if the organization will give him a half-day leave per week in order to attend classes, since some of the classes are during the day. The manager replies that they will give him the half-day leave, but that the degree must be in business studies because sociology is not directly relevant to his job. In this situation the employee has clear constraints upon his actions. If he accepts the offer of leave then he is unable to study his preferred subject. Yet, if he studies his subject of first choice, then he cannot attend all of the classes. Perhaps there are other options, such as finding a course at a different university where all the classes are in the evenings. The employing organization is suggesting a course of action where the employee may find it difficult to act in a genuinely autonomous way, and in which his actions are constrained by their wishes. Such a framework for action, where the individual's choices are limited in this way, is described as heteronomous.

It is a rather difficult philosophical issue whether any decision making, either of an ethical nature or simply of a day-to-day practical nature, can truly be described as autonomous. Decisions can rarely be taken in a social vacuum where there are no limitations on that decision. To some extent it depends upon the particular manner in which we choose to interpret and apply the concept of autonomy. On one level, we are free to take any decision we like. We can break promises as frequently as we like, just as long as we are prepared to face up to the consequences.

see also...
Free Will

Ayer, Alfred J.

Sir Alfred Ayer (1910–89) was a British philosopher who was well known for advocating the logical positivist approach to philosophy. Among the university posts which he held were Grote Professor of the Philosophy of Mind and Logic at London University, and Wykeham Professor of Logic at Oxford University. As with a number of philosophers and thinkers, he to some extent developed his analysis of philosophical issues during his lifetime, but the following represents a summary of his general viewpoint.

In his philosophical writings there was an assumption that there are two main types of statement which can be regarded as truly meaningful. First, analytic propositions which are true because of the meanings of the terms which are employed within the propositions and also because of the logic of the language used in the statements. The scope of such statements is generally regarded as being limited to the propositions of mathematics and of logic.

Then there is a larger category of statements which depend for their verification upon empirical data.

Perhaps the best examples of such statements are to be found in the propositions of the natural sciences such as physics and chemistry. Typically these involve propositions linking precise variables, such as that the size of the electric current in a wire depends partly upon the potential difference between the ends of the wire and also upon the electrical resistance of the wire. Indeed the approach of the physical sciences was a considerable influence upon the general stance of the logical positivist position. Other types of proposition, such as those of metaphysics and religion, were regarded as not being capable of being shown to be either true or false.

The status of ethical propositions was perhaps slightly different, in that a statement such as 'That is not a very civilized way to behave', may be construed as expressing the feeling of the speaker, or as a moral judgement.

see also...

Empiricism; Logical Positivism; Philosophy of Science

Behaviourism

This is a particular approach to the investigation of behaviour which concentrates especially on the use of empirical methods. It was originally a psychological movement associated with the Americans J.B. Watson (1878–1958) and B.F. Skinner (1904–90). The best-known behaviourist research has involved experiments on animals in a laboratory setting. Behaviourists have been interested in exploring the effects of stimuli on animals in carefully controlled situations. Advocates of behaviourism have asserted its objectivity as a method, and sometimes wished to apply the results to human behaviour. Behaviourists are in effect seeking to apply many of the techniques of the natural sciences to the study of behaviour. Critics of behaviourism suggest that what is being examined is only a tiny and insignificant fragment of behaviour patterns – and hence relatively unimportant.

The behaviourist psychologist is not concerned primarily with the nature of the various mental states which might accompany certain patterns of behaviour. As a philosophical position, however, behaviourism assumes that specific mental states accompany specific categories of behaviour. In other words, there is a form of correspondence between mental conditions and behaviour patterns. The main problem deriving from this view is that it is very difficult to conceive how one person can understand the mental states of another, when those must be inferred back from observed or measured behaviour patterns.

Behaviourism as a philosophical position is also a form of reductionism, since the assumption remains that one form of behaviour corresponds to only one type of mental state. In reality, however, it seems much more likely that a particular behaviour pattern results from a complex interaction between a number of different cognitive and environmental factors. The behaviourist tends to be concerned predominantly with the measurable aspects of behaviour.

see also...

Philosophy of Science; Philosophy of the Social Sciences

Categorical Imperative

This is a guideline proposed by the German philosopher Immanuel Kant (1724–1804) to help people to decide on a course of action when they find themselves in an ethical dilemma. The categorical imperative suggests that when we select a course of action, it should be on the assumption that it might become a universal guideline. For example, if when a person bumps into us on a crowded city pavement, we immediately retaliate by pushing them back harder, this would probably lead to a large number of violent confrontations. Hence, it would not be a very good guideline for behaviour and would not comply with the categorical imperative. The ethical criterion, therefore, is whether an act is appropriate for universal application, including to ourselves. If we would not like someone to behave in a certain kind of way towards ourselves, then that is probably an unsuitable manner for us to behave towards others. As a general principle of behaviour, the categorical imperative can seem superficially very persuasive.

However, the main criticism of universal ethical principles is that while they may be laudable in many circumstances, it is not too difficult to imagine exceptional circumstances in which it would possibly be more ethically desirable to contravene the categorical imperative than to comply with it. We might be very happy under normal circumstances to agree that physical violence is wrong, and yet if the lives of our children were threatened by terrorists or criminals, we may be the first to defend them by whatever means was at our disposal. Alternatively, we may argue that it is a universal principle that people should obey the law of the land. Yet, if one of our parents was taken seriously ill we are likely to break the speed limit in driving them to hospital. Again, even though we know it is against the law to break into someone's house, if we witnessed a serious road accident, we might, in the absence of an apparent alternative, consider breaking into someone's house in order to phone for an ambulance. In spite of this criticism, Kant's view retains some appeal.

see also...

Ethics

Causation

Causation explores the meaning of propositions which claim that one event causes another. This may seem such a straightforward issue that it is hardly worth philosophical concern. However, let us consider the issue of human obesity and calorie intake. Here, we might be tempted to suggest that increased calorie intake over a period of time causes obesity. Whilst this may be true for some people, there are others who eat a great deal of food and do not seem to gain weight. Should we therefore begin to wonder whether the increased calories cause the obesity. Perhaps it might be truer to say that there could be an inherent predisposition to obesity, which is linked to our metabolic rate. Perhaps people who put on weight easily have a slower metabolic rate. This then leaves us with a problem over 'cause'. Is the cause the metabolic rate, a hypothetical gene, or the calorie intake or even some other biochemical factor?

Take another example, such as the suggestion that fog causes car accidents. We might say that when there is fog, there appears to be a greater likelihood of car accidents. The difficulty here lies in whether it is accurate to claim that the fog is the 'cause'. In fog it may be that some drivers choose not to slow down sufficiently to compensate for the reduced visibility. It could also be argued that the fog affects a driver's perception. Drivers may respond to fog in different ways. They may assume that the road ahead is clear and that they are relatively safe as long as they are driving steadily. They may become disoriented. Road lights and car lights may appear differently in fog and drivers may be deceived by their appearance. Road lighting may also be inadequate to cope with dense fog. In short, the number of variables makes it difficult to attribute a simple and direct causal link to the notion of fog causing car accidents.

What we can say is that when two events tend to occur closely together, we sometimes make a practical assumption that one event causes the other.

see also...

Necessary Condition; Sufficient Condition

Coherence

The coherence model for determining whether or not an assertion is to be regarded as true, is based upon the idea of comparing it with other related and accepted principles. For example, suppose we are interested in whether computers help schoolchildren to learn. Teachers may carry out some preliminary comparisons and, as a result of these, claim that there is evidence that children with access to their own computer learn more quickly and effectively.

In order to establish the truth or otherwise of this new proposition, the philosopher seeks other propositions which are internally consistent with the aforementioned one. Examples of such propositions might be: children enjoy using computers; children are more motivated when they have a computer; computers teach children transferable skills; and computers help children to integrate their knowledge.

Let us suppose that there is empirical evidence that these propositions are true. If this is so, and if the new proposition that children learn more quickly and effectively with access to a computer is consistent with the above propositions, then we might assume that the new proposition is true. Of course, this line of argument does depend on the meaning which we wish to attribute to the concepts consistent and coherent. Essentially what is being argued is that if the new proposition appears to encapsulate similar ideas which do not contradict the ideas in the pre-existing propositions and appear to be logically related to them, then it is reasonable to assume that the new proposition has the same degree of validity. The coherence theory of truth does not establish the truth of a proposition in an absolute sense, but only provisionally in relation to other propositions. If we extend this principle backwards in time, taking each other proposition in turn, then there is the problem of the way in which the truth of the first proposition was established. Nevertheless the coherence theory of truth does accord with much everyday practice and experience.

see also...

Absolutism; Empiricism; Epistemology; Relativism

Consequence Theories of Ethics

These are ethical theories which argue that the basis for deciding whether an action is to be seen as morally correct or incorrect should be the consequences of that action. In order to explore such theories, let us consider the case of a woman who wins several million pounds in a lottery. She decides that she wants to do something significant with the money. She has a number of relatives who are hoping that they will receive part of the winnings as a gift. The woman thinks about the situation and decides to establish a charitable foundation in a developing country to treat children with leprosy. When she visits potential locations for her charity, she realizes the enormous need of the families in the developing world. She decides that although her relatives are not rich by some European standards, they are very well off compared with people in developing countries. She decides to invest all of her money in her charity and not to give any to her relatives. They are very annoyed at this. They feel that at various times they have supported her, and that she now has the opportunity to make their lives more pleasant. Perhaps we can analyse this situation in terms of consequence theories of ethics.

The first point to make is that consequence theories are of two main types. Some philosophers argue that action A is ethically superior to action B if it tends to result in more happiness. Others suggest that if an action produces more 'goodness', then it is ethically superior to one which generates less goodness. Of course, these suggestions for determining ethical value may raise nearly as many questions as they resolve. For example, happiness is not an easy concept to define or measure, and hence not easy to use as a criterion. Equally, goodness is a very difficult notion about which to be precise. One might even argue that using the term goodness has not resolved the ethical question at all. If we consider the consequences of the woman founding the charitable foundation, one was that the health of a lot of very poor children was improved. Hence, both happiness and goodness were enhanced.

see also...

Ethics; Utilitarianism

Continental Philosophy

It can be argued that during the twentieth century, two broad traditions of philosophy evolved. The one centred upon Britain and the United States has been in the broad tradition of linguistic philosophy. This means that it has been devoted largely to the analysis and clarification of concepts. On the other hand, the tradition centred on continental Europe has been rather different. Although extremely diverse, one of its main features has been an attempt to clarify the position of the individual in relation to the rest of the world, and to explore the response of the individual human being to the dilemmas and challenges of existence. Continental philosophy embraces a number of key thinkers, but as phenomenology and existentialism have been very influential movements, Husserl and Sartre could be regarded as important figures who respectively exemplify these traditions.

Edmund Husserl (1859–1938) was a German philosopher who studied at Berlin and Vienna. He saw the function of philosophy as being to investigate the empirical world, but from the point of view of an analysis of our own thought processes. In everyday life, he argued, we operate in a 'natural' manner treating objects and events in a practical way, often not thinking very much about them. For instance, when we get up to go to work in the morning, we get on a bus or into a car without thinking very much about the concept 'car' or the concept 'bus', unless of course the car will not start or the bus does not arrive. Husserl suggested that we can move from this natural attitude and adopt a phenomenological approach which analyzes what we truly understand by concepts.

Jean-Paul Sartre (1905–80) studied at the Ecole Normale in Paris, and in his early work was influenced by Husserl. Sartre believed that individuals should reflect upon their own position in society and accept responsibility for at least some of the features of their lives. We cannot determine all aspects of our lives, but we can at least consider our circumstances objectively and determine how we wish to develop as human beings.

see also...

Existentialism; Phenomenology

Cosmological Argument

This is one of the commonly advanced arguments for the existence of God. It is also sometimes known as the Causal argument. The starting point of the argument is that the world around us is a varied place with many different events taking place all of the time. Examples of events might be such things as the central heating system breaking down, the discovery of new medicines, and the birth and death of living things. The first logical assumption is that all of these events must have had a cause. The central heating breakdown was perhaps caused by the failure of an electric pump, and the medical discovery resulted at least in part from the skilled judgement of the researcher. Each of these in their turn, it is argued, also had a cause. It should therefore be possible, in principle, to trace backwards a series of causal events, with each prior event causing the subsequent one. Eventually, so the cosmological argument goes, we should arrive at a single original cause which in itself requires no further explanation. The assumption is that the original cause did not result from any previous event. This first cause is regarded as the initiating power of the universe, or what is termed God.

Although the Cosmological argument can be seen as persuasive in its simplicity, it has been subjected to criticisms. A general criticism is that we cannot be certain that all events do have causes. A different, although related criticism, is that the Cosmological argument tends to overlook the complexity of causal links. Such links, it is argued, are not simple and linear but involve a multiplicity of influences. Each event results from a variety of interacting factors.

However, a more specific criticism is that even if there is a first cause, this may arguably be conceptualized as being of a physical, material nature such as, for example, a spontaneous chemical reaction. It does not, so critics argue, need to be thought of as a divine being. It has also been argued that the notion of a first cause which itself is not the result of some pre-existing condition, is very difficult to comprehend and to accept.

see also...

Philosophy of Religion

Critical Theory

A traditional theory in either the natural or the social sciences, attempts to show the relationship between a number of variables, and to both explain these relationships and interactions and also to predict the way in which these variables will interact under future circumstances. To some extent critical theory attempts to achieve all of these, but in addition it sets out to prescribe the way in which the world should be structured or should operate. A critical theory is thus a theory which usually relates to a social science context. Such a theory takes an existing social science situation and tries to demonstrate how a new range of theoretical ideas could have an impact upon that situation. One may speak of 'Critical Theory' as a particular set of analyses, and in this usage the term is usually associated with the Frankfurt School of philosophers and social analysts. Indeed one of the members of that group, Max Horkheimer, is usually credited with initiating the use of the term. However, one may also speak of 'a critical theory' as being a social theory which fulfils certain characteristics.

For example, one might develop a critical theory concerning under-development in the Third World. Such a theory would inevitably wish to challenge some of the traditional assumptions about under-development. It may wish to examine existing economic relations between the First and the Third World; the use of the Third World as a market for goods from the First World; the use of under-developed countries as a pool of inexpensive labour for First World manufacturing industry; the ways in which aid is distributed and the effects which such aid has on the recipient countries. Such a critical theory would develop a range of theoretical concepts which were clearly derived from empirical data and which also were capable of helping to generate practical strategies to improve the situation in developing countries. Moreover, a critical theory should not be considered as a fixed entity, but should be evaluated continually.

see also...

Marx, Karl

Cynicism

This is a belief system which developed in ancient Greece and which is associated with firstly Antisthenes (*c*.445–*c*.360 BCE) and then Diogenes of Sinope (*c*.400–*c*.325 BCE). The Cynics were essentially very dissatisfied with the world as they found it. As they looked around themselves, they found that most apparent sources of pleasure did not bring lasting happiness. Money and material possessions could result in unhappiness if one became preoccupied with them; physical pleasures were only of temporary duration; and contact with other human beings could sometimes make one the victim of unkindness and cruelty. In a perhaps rather pessimistic line of reasoning, the Cynics came to the conclusion that it was contact with other human beings which ultimately led to unhappiness.

Their remedy was that happiness could be found only by withdrawing from the world. Any remaining contact would still run the risk of generating unhappiness. The Cynics tended gradually to adopt the lifestyle of ascetics, living outside the scope of conventional society. They prided themselves in not abiding by the rules of society and in sometimes behaving in an outrageous fashion. To some extent the purpose of the latter was to demonstrate to everyone that they scorned norms and conventions. They tried to shed all possessions in the belief that a simple lifestyle was one which could bring most genuine happiness.

The Cynics argued that they should not seek truth in others but rely on their own individual judgement. There are many obvious parallels with the ascetic traditions in other religions and philosophies. In Buddhism one finds an emphasis on the impermanence of existence and hence a seeking inside oneself for that which does not change; the asceticism of Hindu mendicants has many parallels with Cynicism; and the monastic traditions of many religions share common features. It is rather difficult to establish direct connections, however, and very often similar ideas appear to have evolved independently in different parts of the world.

see also...

Asceticism

De Beauvoir, Simone

Simone de Beauvoir (1908–86) was one of the leading literary figures of the twentieth century : a philosopher, novelist and autobiographical writer. Her *Memoirs of a Dutiful Daughter* and *The Prime of Life* are well-known examples of her autobiographical writing. She wrote the novel *The Mandarins* and in another well-known book, *The Second Sex*, she analyzed the role of women in society. She first met Jean-Paul Sartre in 1929 and they became famous for their intellectual as well as personal relationship. To a certain extent, some features of their philosophical position were reflected in their lives together. She has suggested that for her the concept of marriage would have been an encroachment upon the freedom which she felt that she needed. Marriage would also in a sense have been an unnecessary form of acquiescence to the more conventional norms and values of society. Equally, she appears to have felt that having children would have been a limitation upon her overriding intention to be a writer.

De Beauvoir argued very much for the importance of economic self-sufficiency for women in society. She articulated clearly the arguments for gender equality, and also acknowledged that she was received by Sartre and his colleagues as a full equal. In her philosophical writings on feminism she sought to distinguish between the function of women in terms of their role of bearing children and the roles which they found themselves pressurized to assume through the prevalent definitions of gender in society at large.

A predominant theme of her own life, and indeed of the shared life she had with Sartre, was that of freedom. To her, freedom denoted the capacity to create and then to re-create her own existence, and not to be bound by the value systems and epistemological definitions of traditional society. She viewed female gender not as a biological entity, nor as a psychological condition, but as a social construction. In her view women were encouraged to adapt themselves to societal definitions of femininity.

see also...

Existentialism; Feminism

Deduction

Deduction is a form of reasoning in which the conclusion follows clearly from the original premises. An example of deduction is as follows:

All tennis players hit the ball with a racquet.
Mary is a tennis player.
Therefore Mary hits the ball with a racquet.

If we accept the first two premises, then the conclusion that Mary hits the ball with a racquet must be accepted. We have no choice but to accept the conclusion. It is a valid example of what can be termed deductive logic. In another example we might say:

All tennis players hit their backhand with top-spin.
Mary is a tennis player.
Therefore Mary hits her backhand with top-spin.

This again is a valid example of deductive logic. The conclusion follows from the premises. However, in contrast to the first example, the first premise of the second example is untrue. The fact is that some tennis players slice their backhand, while others might hit it with a flat racquet. Hence it is clear that we can have a valid deductive argument which is based on an incorrect premise. Deductive logic does not make any claims about the veracity of the premises and conclusion, only about the validity of the argument. Incidentally, it is also possible to have premises and a conclusion which are true, but which do not represent valid deduction. For example:

A tennis doubles match involves four players.
Each player serves in turn.
Therefore a serve landing outside the baseline is invalid.

The main criticism of deduction is that as the conclusion is contained in the premises, no new knowledge appears to be generated. This criticism is perhaps more significant for simpler examples of deduction than for more complex ones.

> ### see also...
> *Induction*

Democracy

This is a form of government which entails decision-making, in one way or another, by the people. In its most straightforward form, democracy would entail each member of society voting on an issue. Here we come across the first philosophical issues inherent in democracy. Clearly very young children will not usually be entrusted with voting on weighty issues of state, and there is an issue also about whether a society wishes to establish age or other restrictions on the right of individuals to participate in democratic decision-making. It may also be impractical to have a vote on each and every decision which faces government. Hence democracies tend to be run by elected representatives of the people. In complex democracies it is also problematic whether each individual member of the electorate can appreciate the complexity of the range of issues in contemporary society. This may support the notion of representatives who, as professional politicians, can develop a broader understanding of such matters.

Ethical issues may arise in a democracy when an individual disagrees with laws which are passed by their elected representatives. It is a complex moral and legal issue whether an individual is ever entitled to transgress a law which has been passed within a democratic system. One argument for democracy is that it encourages participation, and yet the practical need to elect representatives results in a system where those representatives have to take many major decisions which were not necessarily evident as issues at the time of election. This emphasizes the importance of the system for electing representatives. It is a matter of practical political importance and also an ethical issue, that the system used to elect representatives generates a group of politicians who most accurately reflect the opinions and will of the electorate. There is a range of different systems and a variety of opinions on how the aim is best achieved. One proposed justification for democracy is that it is arguably the best system for ensuring that the needs of minority groups and disadvantaged groups in society are at least heard and, at best, addressed.

see also...

Mill, John Stuart; Political Philosophy

Deontological Theories

These are a variety of ethical theories linked by a single characteristic – that actions are to be judged as morally right or wrong depending upon the intrinsic nature of the action. According to deontological theories, the morality of actions depends upon their inherent worth. Such theories may be viewed as fundamentally different from consequentialist theories, which as their name suggests, evaluate actions according to the desirability or otherwise of the situations which they produce.

In the case of, say, lying, a deontologist would probably argue that this is always intrinsically wrong. If a person was playing a tennis match and persistently lied about the line calls on his or her side of the net, then that would be seen as wrong. In addition, if a person lied about the mechanical state of a second-hand car to a possible purchaser, then that would also be viewed as wrong. Indeed, both deontologists and consequentialists would probably agree that on both occasions lying was wrong, but for different reasons. Consequentialists would argue that the effects in both cases were undesirable. In the former, the least deserving player wins the game. In the latter, someone purchases a possibly dangerous and unroadworthy vehicle.

However, consider a situation in time of war, when a captured soldier is questioned by his captors. If the captive lies, then he acts unethically in a deontological sense. On the other hand, if he tells the truth when asked questions about his fellow soldiers, then he may place them in peril. In this case he would have acted ethically in a deontological sense, but perhaps unethically in a consequentialist sense. Indeed, deontologists are not totally insensitive to consequences. If the consequences are sufficiently adverse, then deontologists may wish to argue that telling lies is acceptable. Hence deontologists do not necessarily take an absolutely rigid stance on such moral issues.

see also...

Consequence Theories of Ethics;
Utilitarianism

Descartes, Rene

Rene Descartes, the French philosopher (1596–1650), was a very wide-ranging thinker and particularly well-known for his work on a theory of knowledge. His main concern was to try to establish something which he could be absolutely sure was true. He rejected many types of knowledge until he felt he was left with one proposition of which he could be certain. This was that he was sure of his own existence, on the simple grounds that he was a thinking person. If he ever came to doubt the veracity of this, he realized that the very act of doubting was a process of thought – and hence he must exist.

Descartes hoped that if he was correct in his assertion about truth, he would be able to identify a general principle which would help him to know when any other proposition was true. He decided that the key feature of the above proposition which established it as true, was that it was very precise and understandable. He knew exactly what the proposition was claiming.

For Descartes it was often the case that human beings either collect empirical impressions or else they develop their own ideas. Neither of these, he felt, was reliable as a source of knowledge. On the other hand he considered that humans have within themselves the potential to appreciate certain aspects of truth, and that the best example of this was the potential to understand the concept of God. According to Descartes, this concept did not have to be learned but was within us and had only to be appreciated for what it was.

Descartes also considered that the basic concepts of mathematics were within us, and needed only to be realized. On the other hand, the empirical world was regarded as very untrustworthy, and not capable of yielding true knowledge. There is much in the thinking of Descartes that is reminiscent of Plato. This view of knowledge has been challenged on the grounds that there is no independent proof that these intrinsic ideas actually exist in the form suggested by Descartes.

see also...

Epistemology

Determinism

This is the view that each event in the world has been pre-ordained by virtue of previous events and the general rules by which the universe functions. According to its adherents, determinism is affected first by the existence of a range of physical and chemical processes in the universe which act consistently. We may not understand all of these, but there is the assumption that they are operating all the time. An example might be the principle of gravity. Second there is the assumption that every event has a cause or causes. Hence, determinists argue that if a situation is created involving certain specific factors, and there are certain physical laws operating, then there is only one outcome which can result. For many determinists there are no such things as chance occurrences. Everything happens because of the pre-existing circumstances. If such were the case, one would assume that it was possible to predict all future events – when clearly it is not. Determinists argue that, in principle, it is possible, but it is simply the case that at any given time we are not aware of all of the factors that are operating.

The implications of determinism for human conduct, morality and free will are enormous. Suppose, for example, that a person is deciding whether to go on an expensive holiday or, alternatively, to go on a cheaper one and to give some money to charity. Some may argue that this is simply a matter of the person exercising their own free will. Some determinists, however, would say that taking into account the genetic make-up of the individual and his or her upbringing, that only one decision is possible.

A strict interpretation of determinism tends to suggest that individuals cannot be responsible for the morality of their actions. If all events and personal decisions are in a sense pre-ordained, then individuals may not seem to be morally responsible for them. Also, it may be difficult to have aspirations in one's personal life if, as a strict determinist, one assumes that one has little if any control over the future.

see also...

Free Will

Dewey, John

John Dewey (1859–1952) was a very influential American philosopher, well known for his application of theoretical philosophical ideas to the practical issues of his day. In particular, he contributed to the debate on politics and education, and is still referred to frequently in contemporary discussion on educational issues. Dewey began his education at the University of Vermont, but as an academic he is perhaps best known for the period from 1894 onwards when he taught at the University of Chicago, and then later at the University of Columbia. While at Chicago he founded an innovative school from which evolved many of his ideas on educational systems.

For Dewey, the search after knowledge was not a matter of trying to acquire a fixed and final version of reality, but of engaging in a process which saw knowledge as an ongoing means of developing understanding. In addition, knowledge could be understood only in the context of its application to practical situations.

Dewey's view of the ideal society was one in which each individual could bring his or her unique abilities to contribute to the development of society. It was this process of development which was central to his concept of education. Dewey believed that an education system was not a mechanism for simply transmitting knowledge to young people. Although he saw the cultural inheritance of humanity as being very important, he thought it essential to focus upon the process of educational development. Hence, children should be encouraged to think for themselves, to apply principles of analysis to new contexts, and to be able to use ideas rather than simply accumulate knowledge. In this way, he suggested children would be better able to respond to a rapidly changing future. It is easy to appreciate how Dewey's ideas have either directly or indirectly influenced some contemporary educational thinking, particularly the widespread current trend of trying to teach young people transferable, analytic skills rather than concentrating on the rather passive acquiring of factual information.

see also...

Philosophy of Education

Dialectic

This is a process of reasoning designed to gradually clarify, and then to resolve an issue. It was originally associated with Socrates who used the dialectical approach to attempt to reveal something of the truth of a problem. This approach usually involves a carefully structured question and answer technique, which does not necessarily assume any knowledge on the part of the individual being questioned. The latter is gradually brought to an understanding of the issue, as the logical pattern of questioning helps the individual to systematize his or her thoughts. The so-called Socratic method has become well known in education as an effective way to teach. Its advocates argue that it helps students to learn because it does not simply give them information, but helps them to think critically about an issue.

The German philosopher Georg Hegel (1770–1831) adapted the idea of the dialectic and, as a result, it became a very influential notion and a central component of the philosophy of Karl Marx (1818–83). Hegel viewed the dialectic as a fundamental form of analysis in the world. To take a contemporary example of a car not starting, someone may suggest that the reason is a flat battery. In Hegelian terms, this proposal is the 'thesis'. Another person may then observe that the car lights are working and argue that there is nothing wrong with the battery. In Hegel's terms this is the 'antithesis'. Out of this emerges a new idea about a possible cause – this is the 'synthesis'. The latter then becomes, in effect, the new thesis for the next cycle of analysis. The process continues until an accepted synthesis is reached, representing an agreed explanation for the car not starting.

Hegel also argued that this cyclical process of thesis – antithesis – synthesis, can be used to explain the course of history. A nation with a particular political structure constitutes the thesis. Another nation which is in conflict with this system then arises. This constitutes the antithesis. There is then a struggle and the resulting state represents the synthesis.

see also...
Marx, Karl

Egoism

This term represents a range of philosophical positions which share the feature of actions relating primarily to self-interest. As with most philosophical approaches there is a continuum of terms which may all be loosely described as versions of egoism, but which represent divergent positions. Egoism may first be used as a descriptive term for the approach of an individual whose actions clearly appear to be related to the satisfaction or promotion of the self. In business, people who are always saying how wonderfully they have performed or achieved could be described as egoistic. On a bus or train, people who push ahead of others to try to make sure that they get a seat could also be described as egoistic. One could assume that such people do have an alternative and are capable of choosing to act differently. Hence, they could be described as being motivated by egoism. A different scenario is envisaged where we assume that individuals cannot help acting egoistically because it is part of their psychological nature. In this case there is no ethical choice involved because the individual is not in a position to reflect upon the action taken.

The opposite of egoism is altruism, where individuals select actions which are primarily intended to further the welfare of others rather than themselves. However, egoism and altruism can overlap as in the case of a person who acts egoistically on the assumption that in the long term he will be better able to help others. Consider the case of a person who wishes to become a social worker. He may decide that he must first establish himself in a reasonable home with a secure income so that he will be free of material concerns and more able to help others. Such a person may argue that he can scarcely be in a position to help others when he has continual worries about a place to live and adequate income.

A further variant is when a person acts in what appears to be an altruistic sense, but where such altruism gives him egoistic satisfaction.

see also...

Ethics

Emotive Theory

Suppose that we are observing a school playground and we see several boys teasing and bullying a smaller boy. Eventually the smaller boy bursts into tears and runs away, leaving the older boys laughing at him. When we see this, we feel an immediate revulsion. We do not need to work out whether such behaviour is morally wrong; we just know that it is. We want to shout out how awful it is and that the older boys should be punished. The emotive theory of ethics represents the view that moral judgements are fundamentally an articulation of our feelings, such as 'I think that's good' or 'I don't think that's fair.'

It is perhaps at this stage worth distinguishing between the general cognitivist approach to ethics which sees ethical statements as capable of being evaluated as right or wrong; and the non-cognitivist approach which sees moral judgements as incapable of being evaluated in the above manner. The emotive theory is clearly non-cognitivist. If moral statements are to be reduced to the level of an indication of feelings about an issue, then it is clearly going to be difficult to evaluate and to compare such propositions.

In support of the emotive theory, it does tend to accord with many aspects of our everyday discourse about moral issues. We tend to make our minds up very quickly on a question, relying often on our intuitive feelings. However, there are several disadvantages with the emotive approach. Different people may have very different feelings about an issue and there may be no apparent means of comparison. Moreover, the emotive theory may seem reasonable if we have access to a wide range of opinions about a particular question, and also if we can make up our own minds about it fairly easily. However, if this is not the case, then it may be rather difficult to resolve the matter. The emotive theory does not provide us with any real means of assessing a moral dilemma. We have no way of trying to analyze objectively a moral question and of trying to resolve it.

see also...

Ethics; Utilitarianism

Empiricism

This is a theory about how we come to have knowledge about the world. The view of empiricists is that we gain knowledge through our senses such as our eyes, ears, and sense of touch. Empirical data upon which our knowledge is based can therefore take many forms. An engineer who is trying to work out why a washing machine has broken down, builds up empirical knowledge through a series of electrical and mechanical tests. An ornithologist acquires an understanding of the behaviour of birds through hours of careful empirical observation. A piano tuner uses empirical data gained through listening to re-tune a piano.

One of the early advocates of empiricism was the philosopher John Locke (1632–1704) whose perhaps best-known work was *Essay concerning Human Understanding*. Since that time the empirical approach to knowledge has become more and more predominant. We can readily see its influence within our educational system. Students are continually encouraged to make and record observations, and then to seek patterns in those observations. There is much evidence of this approach in laboratory science lessons and in geography field trips. In subjects such as history, also, old documents and artefacts are referred to as empirical data, partly because they can be studied through observation. The philosophical approach of empiricism was particularly significant in the rise of the scientific approach to life and we can see the best examples of empiricism in present-day science and engineering.

An alternative philosophical position is that of the Rationalist philosophers. They argue that knowledge is gained mainly by analyzing ideas in our minds, rather than through observation. The popularity of empiricism, however, is possibly based on the idea that it provides a philosophical basis for a very practical approach to human existence. The prime criticism has come from those who suggest that observations do not reveal knowledge of the world.

see also...

A Priori, Epistemology; Rationalism

Epicureanism

picurus, a Greek philosopher (342–270 BCE) established a philosophical approach which was characterized as much by a particular style of living, as by its philosophical claims. He founded a school at Athens which he called 'The Garden', and gathered around himself a group of people who adhered to the principles of the simple, rather ascetic life recommended by Epicurus. Membership of the group was open to both women and men and people from all strata of society.

The essential philosophy of Epicurus consisted of the pursuit of happiness, yet this was not a happiness to be gained by attempting to live a life of luxury or one devoted to material pleasures. The members of an Epicurean group aimed to live a life of simplicity, providing mutual support for each other, and trying as far as possible to avoid the unpleasant features of life. As part of this strategy they tended to avoid involvement in the social and political issues of the day, devoting themselves to the peaceful, meditative life of their community. Epicureans tried to live as pleasurable a life as possible. Their strategy for achieving this was to provide the body with just the basic requirements of nutrition and to live a simply, healthy life. There was also an emphasis upon gaining a peaceful state of mind. They encouraged a rational approach to the anxieties of living, and an attempt to create a relatively calm and peaceful way of life.

It is perhaps unfortunate that Epicureans became associated with a singularly hedonistic lifestyle. It is true that they saw happiness as the chief good in life, but this was not a happiness to be gained by the unqualified pursuit of worldly pleasures – in fact, quite the opposite. The simplicity of life advocated by the Epicureans has many parallels, including that of communities of Buddhist monks. One of the major concerns for any group of people who withdraw from the worldly life, is how to support themselves. There is sometimes a conflict between the need to be self-supporting and the wish to reject society.

see also...
Asceticism

Epistemology

This is the branch of philosophy which is concerned with procedures by which we come to claim that something is true. For example, we are told many things on television, which we are invited to believe are true. Such examples might include a group which has climbed a previously unconquered peak in the Himalayas; someone who has sailed around the world; or a rocket that has landed a remote-controlled device on one of the planets of our solar system. These claims are usually supported by video footage and interviews with some of the participants, once they have completed their achievements. This discussion is not to suggest that some of this type of evidence might be contrived. However, as philosophers we must step back and ask ourselves on what grounds we are prepared to accept these statements as true. Such questions are epistemological questions.

Throughout the history of philosophy, there have been two broad schools of thought on such questions. The so-called rationalists have suggested that it should be possible to identify certain types of knowledge based purely upon mental analysis and without recourse to observations of the world around us. An example of such knowledge might be the role of a creator in the establishment of the universe. Philosophers who took a largely rationalistic approach include the German philosopher Gottfried Leibniz (1646–1716) and the French philosopher Rene Descartes (1596–1650). Other philosophers, the empiricists, have argued that true knowledge can be derived only from data collected by our senses. In other words our observations of our surroundings form the only certain basis for knowing whether something is true or false. Philosophers particularly associated with empiricism include the English philosopher John Locke (1632–1704) and the Scottish philosopher David Hume (1711–76). A compromise between these broad schools is that empirical data requires analysis in order to systematize it.

> ## *see also...*
>
> *A Prior; Empiricism; Logical Positivism; Rationalism*

Essentialism

Imagine that a vintage car in very poor condition is being taken apart by a group of mechanics in order to rebuild and renovate it. The car in its present condition is very rusty but has all of the component parts present. As they take it apart bit by bit, the car is still recognizable as a car. They remove the windows and windscreen, and it is still clearly a car. The doors come off next, and although the car is now looking a little skeletal, it is obviously still a car. Next they remove the bonnet and lift out the engine. The car would still be recognizable as a car. However, the process continues until eventually all that remains on the floor of the garage are the axles and four wheels. This is by now not a car! It is four wheels joined together. The philosophical point here is that there must have been a stage in taking the car apart when most people would have been happy to agree that it was still a car – but only just. When something else was removed, it ceased to be a car, and simply became some spare motor vehicle components.

The purpose of this discussion is to investigate whether there are some components of a car which must be in place for it still to be recognized in the public domain as a car. Essentialism is the view that it is possible for any object or person to define certain attributes which must be in existence for the original identity to be retained. Thus, in the case above, we may not regard wing mirrors as an essential attribute of a car. Many cars have their wing mirrors knocked off by other vehicles passing too close, but they still retain their identity as a car. A wing mirror, then, could be termed an incidental attribute of a car, rather than an essential attribute.

It is interesting to reflect on how we come to regard certain attributes as essential and others as incidental. It may arise to some extent from the way in which concepts are partly defined through the process of inter-subjective agreement by individuals. In terms of, say, the concept 'dog', we come to understand which instances of mammals may be included within this category and which may not.

see also...

Necessary Condition; Sufficient Condition

Ethics

A woman is selling her house to a newly married, young couple. She explains to them the problems with the house in terms of structure and function. However, there are some disadvantages of living in this particular house which only an experienced home-owner might realize in advance of purchase. These will not entail expenditure for the purchasers, but they may not be as satisfied with the house as they anticipated. The woman ponders on what she should tell the couple. She herself would like to sell the house fairly quickly and on the one hand does not feel inclined to reveal things which a reasonably perceptive purchaser would consider. On the other hand, she remembers how inexperienced she was when buying her own first house, and feels a responsibility to be as open as she can. This is an example of an ethical problem. It is not perhaps the most serious type of problem we would ever face, but most ethical issues are by their nature very complex.

Ethical problems are those which involve a decision about how we ought to behave. The word 'ethics' can be used in slightly different ways.

It can be used rather like 'morality' or moral principles, to indicate a set of values by which people live. It can be used to signify the principles of right and wrong which a particular society has developed to order its existence. Philosophers use the term more specifically to indicate an area of study which is concerned with establishing what people are trying to say when they make statements prescribing a particular kind of behaviour. As a part of this, ethics is also the study and analysis of the 'grand theories' proposed by philosophers concerning the way in which they advocate people conducting their lives.

There are many grand theories of ethics. Plato, for example, considered that the nature of goodness, and hence of the capacity to lead a moral life, was knowledge which was potentially available to all.

---

see also...

Consequence Theories of Ethics;
Deontological Theories;
Utilitarianism

Existentialism

Existentialists are concerned with resolving a range of philosophical questions about the nature of human beings and our relationship to the world. They are interested in such fundamental questions as the nature of human existence, the purpose of our existence, and the ways in which we might best live our lives. In other words, existentialists address questions which while having a lot of theoretical philosophical importance, are also very important, practical matters for non-philosophers. Particularly associated with existentialism are the Danish philosopher Soren Kierkegaard (1813–55), and the French philosophers Jean-Paul Sartre (1905–80) and Simone de Beauvoir (1908–86).

Existentialists represent a broad range of philosophical beliefs and claims, but in general they are associated with the notion of doubt about whether it is possible to definitely know anything about the world. This lack of certainty can be very disconcerting for human beings and the only solution is to determine to believe in something. This act of belief is seen as being important in giving a meaning to life and may entail a decision to believe in God, or to believe in a moral or political principle. Existentialists typically assert that it is very difficult as human beings to know that we have chosen the right belief system, but all we can do is to have faith in our choice, and then to live by that choice as best we can. When it comes to making a decision to follow a specific world view, this may or may not involve faith in a religious sense.

Existentialists are particularly concerned about the situation in which human beings find themselves in a world which is unpredictable and full of often unsatisfactory events. At the same time, there is a great sense of freedom for human beings. We live in a world of enormous variety in terms of political systems, religious systems and belief systems. The dilemma for human beings is how to orientate ourselves within such diversity.

see also...

De Beauvoir, Simone; Kierkegaard, Soren

Feminism

In philosophical terms feminism is concerned that historically philosophy has become pervaded by styles of thinking and reasoning which are associated, rightly or wrongly, with masculinity. Some argue that there has been the general assumption that while masculinity is related to the application of rationality, logic, mathematics and regulatory principles, femininity has been associated with emotional forms of argument. Of course, one can argue that the emotions are as significant a basis for the generation of knowledge as is the application of reason.

There are two arguments which may be made here. First, if there is some validity in the thesis that there are distinctively male and female ways of looking at the world and generating knowledge about it, then one can argue that female thinkers have been placed at the sidelines of a discipline which focuses on masculine approaches to analysis. Second, if there are no substantive differences between the approaches to thinking and analysis of men and women, then it would be doing a disservice to women to assume that they look at the world only from an emotional viewpoint. In this case it may be argued that women are being unfairly treated by being in effect excluded from the mainstream of philosophical thought.

In addition, feminist philosophers argue that from the wide range of concerns which could be addressed by philosophers, those that are of particular concern to women have been substantially ignored. These might include such issues as the under-representation of women in a large number of professions, and the social roles occupied by women.

In relation to these issues is the fundamental feminist concern with the process of analysis whereby a woman's role is defined. This is both a sociological and a philosophical process. In philosophical terms, feminists generally argue that the concept of 'woman' has been analyzed and specified by men, and what is required is a re-analysis of that concept by women.

see also...

De Beauvoir, Simone; Ethics

Free Will

The problem of free will has generally been viewed as whether human beings are genuinely free to make autonomous decisions, or whether they are constrained in some way. Clearly most societies have evolved various norms and customs which define which kind of actions are acceptable in a particular circumstance, and it may be very difficult in both a psychological and sociological sense not to comply with those norms. For example, in time of war it would not be easy for someone to claim exemption from enlisting on the grounds of firmly held religious convictions. The general debate, however, in a philosophical sense, has been to clarify whether human beings have a genuine free will if the universe is deterministic. If determinism is true, then given the general physical laws and principles which govern the universe, and given also a certain set of circumstances preceding a particular event, then determinists argue that there will be only one particular version of that event which can occur. If determinism is true then it does tend to preclude the possibility of free will and autonomous moral actions because these have in a sense already been decided.

There are two general ways in which we can address this problem. The first, and perhaps the most straightforward, is to deny the validity of determinism. Even though there is a certain logic to the arguments of the determinists, it is not possible to confirm their assertions and to predict future events based upon our knowledge of existing circumstances. Hence some advocates of a genuine free will may suggest that there is no real philosophical problem since the validity of determinism cannot be verified.

The second argument is that if determinism is valid, then this does not necessarily pose a problem for free will. The argument rests upon an alleged confusion over the nature of freedom. It is suggested that even if all actions are predetermined, this just means that there is a tendency towards one event rather than another.

see also...

Determinism

Functionalism

Within the philosophy of social science, functionalism is a sociological perspective which raises interesting philosophical questions. If we imagine the human body and the different organ systems which make it up, it is relatively easy to analyze these systems in terms of their function. There is a circulatory system, a nervous system and a digestive system. All of these systems have a particular function and their constituent parts are adapted to carry out these functions. Functionalist sociologists apply this analysis to society at large, where they might suggest that a financial system, manufacturing system, judicial system, and civil service, all fulfil important functional roles in society. In the case of the human body the assumption is that in a healthy person all of the biological systems work together to produce a coordinated organism. Similarly, functionalist sociologists suggest that these different social systems combine together to ensure the effective integration of society. There is, however, an important philosophical question here about whether a biological system is analogous to a social system.

The education system within a society is perhaps a case in point. We may think of an education system as furthering consensus in society, by helping to ensure that there is an educated and trained workforce and that each individual is able to play his or her part in the economic future of society. Some sociologists argue that this version of consensus needs to be modified because education can sometimes result in disharmony. Discontent may arise, for example, if a person has studied hard and gained a degree, only to find themselves unemployed because of insufficient jobs due to economic factors in society. Equally well, the education system could be seen as encouraging stratification in society, by financially rewarding those with qualifications, and leaving many others without qualifications as unemployed.

The validity or otherwise of these competing claims about the function of education, is partly an epistemological question.

see also...

Philosophy of the Social Sciences

Hedonism

This is the doctrine that the pursuit of pleasure is the most appropriate goal for human beings. Hedonism can be viewed as either a psychological theory or an ethical theory. In a psychological sense it argues that human behaviour can be best explained by viewing human beings as motivated primarily by the desire for pleasure. In other words, when confronted by a decision of whether to do X or Y, an individual will generally select the option which is considered likely to bring the most pleasure. In terms of an ethical theory, hedonism argues that it is a desirable thing for human beings to pursue pleasure. It is thus a consequentialist theory of ethics, in that actions are judged on the basis of the amount of pleasure they are likely to create. Both uses of the term raise a number of philosophical questions about the idea of pleasure. Some people may interpret hedonism with being simply concerned with seeking pleasure for themselves. Others may interpret it as the desire for pleasure for a wider number of people. There are thus questions to be resolved about those who are intended to benefit from the seeking of pleasure.

Another philosophical question raised by hedonism is that of the nature of pleasure. Some may interpret the term as referring to physical pleasures, while others may think of pleasure in terms of peace and tranquility. Clearly, that which is pleasurable to one person, may not appeal to another. Moreover there are some activities which, while bringing about temporary pleasure, may in the long run bring unhappiness. Eating rich food may be pleasant at the time, but may result in illness later. If one is advocating an ethical theory of hedonism, therefore, it is important to clarify the nature of the pleasure which should be pursued. Is one advocating physical pleasures or more cerebral pleasures?

Finally, if it is being argued that we ought to pursue pleasure, is it possible to evaluate pleasure objectively? It is necessary to consider whether it is possible to compare the pleasures of convivial company, with the pleasure of playing sport or of academic study.

see also...

Epicureanism; Utilitarianism

Heidegger, Martin

Martin Heidegger (1889–1976) was a German philosopher who worked at the universities of Freiburg and Marburg. He is perhaps best known for his analysis of the nature of existence. For Heidegger, the term 'existence' signifies both the way in which individual people understand the nature of their own being, and also the way in which other people recognize us as 'being'. Heidegger viewed existence not as a permanent entity but rather as a dynamic process through which each individual is capable of relating to the world and to other people throughout their whole life. Existence is a process which has to relate to the social environment in which it finds itself. Thus a person may apply for and obtain a new job, yet find that the new working environment is not very relaxing or conducive to a productive working life. The individual may not quickly be able to escape from this environment because of the need to make a living, and hence the nature of existence has to cope with this context.

Life is full of choices and we do not always know the direction in which some of these choices will take us. Nevertheless, the choices which we make define the parameters of our existence and make a statement to the world about how we perceive the nature of our own being. For instance, the way in which we inter-relate with our colleagues in the work-place, says something about our appreciation of our fellow human beings in a context which is at times difficult and stressful.

Heidegger felt that it is all too easy for individuals to fit in with the prevailing norms of society even when they have an overwhelming desire to take a stand on a particular issue. He considered it important that each individual, if necessary, should be prepared to make a practical statement which would convert their philosophical reflections into a public manifestation of their existence and being.

see also...

Existentialism

Hermeneutics

When we read a historical text, particularly one which was written at least several centuries ago and within a different culture, it is often very difficult to understand the full meaning of the text. If it is a descriptive account of a historical event, such as a meeting or a battle, then we may be tempted to think that the account is straightforward in a factual sense. This may not always be the case. The science and art of interpreting the meaning of historical texts is termed hermeneutics. The term is generally associated with attempts to understand the biblical scriptures and to analyze the ways in which, for example, the accounts of the life of Jesus differ. Hermeneutics as a term, however, can be applied not only to biblical exegesis but also generally to attempts to understand and interpret texts. Problems of interpretation are particularly significant in relation to historical texts where we do not have the possibility of consulting people who may have been alive at the time the text was written.

When scholars use hermeneutic techniques to analyze historical documents, there are a number of factors which they need to take into account. The writer will have written the text within a particular cultural framework, conditioned partly by such factors as his or her social class, education, family background and relationship to those who held political power at the time. In writing an account of a war or of a political conflict, the writer may have been torn between a wish to produce a factual historical account, and a desire not to alienate the existing power elites. In some societies the support of the latter may have been essential if the writer was to avoid persecution or even death. In most cases the researcher will have access to a range of data which can shed light on the textual account and its cultural context. This may include archaeological evidence, inscriptions on contemporary buildings, and other textual material.

see also...

Meaning

Historicism

Let us suppose that the course of history was to some extent preordained and that it was destined to develop in a certain way. Perhaps we might assume that one type of economic system would inevitably follow another type; or that political systems tended to develop in a certain sequence. This type of assumption about the evolution of history is termed historicism. This view of historicism also tends to be associated with the assertion that human beings cannot substantially alter the course of history. The inevitability of the process precludes human intervention. This perception of historicism has difficulty explaining how key figures in history have managed to have such an impact. In the case of, say, the decline of the British Empire and colonialism, a historicist may argue that it bore within it the seeds of its own decline. In other words, whatever men and women did, there was little that could be done to support such a system. Opponents of historicism would argue that the decline would have at least been slowed down and may not have taken place, if it had not been for the intervention of such people as Gandhi in India. Although it is possibly true that colonial systems have within them a potential disequilibrium caused in part by the fundamental unethical and exploitative nature of the relationship, it could be argued that it requires the intervention of a unique individual to act as a focus for the redistribution of political power. Historicists, of course, may retort that the arrival of such individuals at key times in history is a feature of the very historical process they are talking about.

Another aspect of the general historicist view is that historical events must be considered and analyzed within their contemporary framework and not within the parameters of modern times. An example might be the ethics of the way warfare was conducted in the ancient world, and the way prisoners and slaves were treated. On an individual level, we may find this excessively cruel. A historicist may argue, however, that it should be viewed within the perspective of the limited life expectancy of the time.

see also...

Relativism

Hobbes, Thomas

Thomas Hobbes (1588–1679) was an English philosopher known particularly for his contribution to political philosophy. He lived through the period of the English Civil War and supported King Charles, although not unequivocally. The political philosophy of Thomas Hobbes focused upon the issue of the mechanism by which the state should be governed, and whether it was possible to balance the advantages of rule by a single person, with preserving the liberties of individual citizens. Hobbes believed that if people were left to govern themselves without powerful leadership, then there would normally be a tendency for factions to develop and to compete against each other. Such disputes would lead to an unstable society in which the liberties of individuals would be threatened by the general disregard for firm laws. Different groups would pursue wealth and power and this would lead to disharmony and conflict in society.

Hobbes felt that the best way to guard against this was to have strong leadership, and on balance he favoured rule by a single person. Such a ruler would be responsible for establishing all of the laws in society, and individual citizens would have an obligation to comply with those laws. If several people ruled together, there would inevitably be disagreements at times, leading once again to disharmony. However, Hobbes agreed that measures were necessary to ensure that individual liberties were not excessively transgressed. For example, the ruler had an obligation to protect all citizens, and although he or she could require citizens to engage in a dangerous war to protect the state, this was not reasonable if the war was to exercise aggression against a neighbouring state. Hobbes felt that there were also general obligations upon citizens to minimize the risk of crime, and to do their best to thwart attempts to break the law.

The principal criticism of Hobbes is that it is a system which, through its attempts to safeguard against the risk of anarchy in society, rests power in the hands of a single person.

see also...

Political philosophy

Holism

When we watch a successful soccer team mount an attack on the opposition, we can sometimes get the feeling that the team as a whole exhibits qualities greater than those of the individual players. The way the team passes the ball and anticipates the position of other players, suggests a collaborative quality which is unique to that group of players. The way in which a team works together, somehow exceeding the talents of the individual members, is an example of holism.

The concept of holism can be applied in a variety of different contexts. In biology for example, it is becoming increasingly possible to explain the functioning of living things at the chemical level. The more explanation operates at this level, however, the greater the danger that we lose sight of the sophistication of the whole organism. In the case of human beings, we may be able to replace parts of the body and remedy biochemical deficiencies, but the individual human being is still capable of very complex responses. For example, human beings are capable of risking their own lives for others, and of evaluating complex ethical dilemmas. This does lead us to wonder whether a reductionist explanation of the human being at the level of chemical processes, misses something of the complex nature of humans. Holists would tend to adopt the view that living things do exhibit patterns of behaviour which cannot simply be reduced to the lowest common denominator of biochemistry.

Much the same argument can be used of human society. When groups of human beings come together, linked by a number of common features, the holist would argue that collectively they exhibit certain characteristics which are absent in the individual. For example, when a person trains for a particular job, it is not simply a matter of acquiring certain skills, but usually of learning a range of norms and conventions which apply to that profession. We learn that under certain circumstances we are expected to behave in a certain way.

see also...

Essentialism

47

Humanism

This is the general belief system which suggests that there exists inherent goodness and nobility in the human spirit, and seeks to make these qualities the focus for action in the world. The development of humanism may be associated with a gradual assumption that God plays a less and less central role in the general scheme of things. In the Renaissance, society very slowly began to move from a view that held God in direct control of all aspects of existence, to a position where human beings were viewed by some as potentially capable of being in control of their own existence. This philosophical position provided a framework within which the growth of empirical science could begin to develop, since God was no longer seen by all as being necessarily the determinant of events.

A further stage in the development of humanism took place with the implicit challenge to religious tradition provided by the work of Charles Darwin. Living things were no longer seen as being subject to divine control, but to processes which were explicable in empirical and rational terms. Unless one retained a view of God as the supreme power in the universe, there was by now a natural tendency to look for the good and the noble in the hearts and minds of human beings.

A clear theme in humanism has been the application of reason to the problems of the world, rather than to seek divine guidance. However, some humanists have been unhappy with the view that science and technology can solve all of the difficulties of the world. The expansion of technology and the effects of this on the lives of human beings is seen by some as having a de-humanizing effect. In addition, the demands upon natural resources made by large-scale industrialization, are not viewed by many as advancing the cause of humanism. Humanists prefer to give a central role to ethical value in the decision-making process about the way the world should develop. Hence, humanists have tended to take clear moral positions upon such issues as conditions in developing countries.

see also...

Epistemology; Ethics; Philosophy of Religion

Hume, David

David Hume (1711–76) was a Scottish philosopher, well known for his scepticism in relation to the extent to which human beings could attain certainty in knowledge. He sought to analyze carefully in all areas of philosophy, the limits and constraints upon what we are capable of knowing. After studying initially at the University of Edinburgh, he went to live in France. In later life he became the Librarian to the Faculty of Advocates in Edinburgh. His works include: *An Enquiry concerning Human Understanding*; *A Treatise of Human Nature* and *An Enquiry concerning the Principles of Morals*.

One of the problems Hume addressed was the extent to which we can be certain about future instances of events that we can currently observe, or which we have observed in the past. For example, it may be that for as long as we can remember, we have observed an oak tree in our garden losing its leaves in the Autumn. However, the problem raised by Hume was whether we could ever be certain that there might come a year when the oak tree might keep its leaves right through the winter.

Hume's argument was that we cannot rely on either logical thought processes nor upon empirical experience to tell us absolutely that the tree will always lose its leaves in future. There is no way we can establish absolute certainty of this.

Hume was generally rather doubtful about the existence of an independent 'self' in each human being. He felt that belief in this was somewhat of a delusion. Human beings experience and interpret a complex range of observations about the world, and in a sense this constitutes what we might commonly refer to as the self. He was also very doubtful about the possibility of establishing the validity of causal connections. No matter how carefully one felt one had established that a particular event caused another, Hume argued that there were always limits to that certainty.

see also...
Epistemology; Induction; Scepticism

Idealism

This is the view that when we consider the nature of the world around us, the ultimate reality appears to exist in our minds rather than in the material world. Idealists attach varying degrees of reality to the material world, ranging from the notion that only minds exist, to the argument that although the material world is important, mental processes are required to interpret it. If we imagine the simple example of a book having been placed on a table, common sense indicates that the book definitely exists. We can see it, touch it, and leaf through the pages. Idealists would argue, however, that any attempt to appreciate the reality of the book is ultimately mental. All the features of the book which are transmitted to us through empirical processes, are evaluated mentally before we come to a judgement about the book. For example, we can feel the texture of the paper, and form a judgement about its quality. We can observe the condition of the binding, and decide on the approximate age of the book. We can, of course, read the book, and interpret the ideas. In other words, idealists suggest that all of the judgements we make are the result of mental processes.

Non-idealists (or materialists, as they are usually known) would argue that if we imagined a universe in which there were no minds, then the book would still exist. It would have exactly the same characteristics. Admittedly, there would be no minds there to perceive the book, but presumably the book would still be there on the table! An idealist may concede this point, but might go on to argue that although the book is still on the table, there would be no one to conceptualize it as a book. The pieces of paper and cardboard could simply be fuel for a fire, or perhaps a doorstop! It is only a book because perceptive, rational minds classify a collection of bound paper with printing on it, as such.

Different versions of idealism have been advocated by, among others, Plato (*c*. 427–347 BCE) and Bishop George Berkeley (1685–1753).

see also...

A Priori

Induction

Induction is a process of logical reasoning whereby we derive a general rule from a number of observations of a phenomenon. An everyday example of induction would be that if we kept cats as pets for a long period of time, and observed that they all liked to sleep by the fire, then we might propose a generalization that all cats like to sleep by the fire. We can express the process of inductive reasoning more generally by saying that if all observed As have a particular characteristic, then all other As will also possess that characteristic. This type of reasoning process has clear importance in research and science, where researchers carefully collect empirical observations and then seek to produce a generalization or scientific principle from these observations which has much wider applicability.

Many philosophers (notably David Hume) have argued that there is a fundamental problem with the principle of induction. This is that there is no justification for considering a range of observable instances and then proposing that all similar instances, which might be observed elsewhere or in the future, will be identical. Of course, on a common sense level, it is very tempting to do this, because we are surrounded with so many patterns in nature which appear to be predictable. Daffodils bloom in springtime and the stars appear in predictable constellations. We are therefore very much inclined to induce that daffodils will for ever and a day blossom in spring, and the constellation of Orion the hunter will always have the same shape. The problem of induction emphasizes that we cannot logically always be absolutely certain that such observable patterns will continue into the future. As with most philosophical processes, however, induction is rarely a straightforward or simple process. The empirical data upon which the principle is based, is rarely totally uniform. The result of this is that someone may base generalizations on some of the data, but not all of it. It is perhaps important in the interests of thoroughness and analytic rigour that one should continually examine the generalizations resulting from induction.

see also...

Deduction

Instrumentalism

Let us suppose that a gardener has developed a special way of making garden compost and that he spreads it around his rose bushes every year. The roses bloom magnificently and the gardener claims that it is because of the special compost. The gardener may not understand the mechanism by which the compost allegedly works, but he always stands by his theory that it is the compost which helps to produce the splendid blooms. As evidence to support his theory, he cites the case of his next door neighbour who does not have the advantage of the special compost and whose roses produce only rather ordinary flowers. The claim that the compost has special nutritional value and helps produce excellent roses is an everyday example of an instrumental theory. Such a theory is largely supported by the evidence that it 'appears' to work and have practical application. There is not, however, the kind of additional empirical evidence which one would normally expect.

Philosophers who subscribe to an instrumentalist view of scientific theories argue that a theory should be judged primarily by the extent to which it can be used for a practical purpose. Hence, one can accept a theory in an instrumentalist sense, while still reserving opinion upon whether it can be accepted in a broader sense, and regarded as verified. Part of the difficulty in distinguishing between these two levels of proof is that they are not completely distinct in practical terms. For example, one of the main criteria for establishing the veracity of a theory is the extent to which it actually can be applied in the real world. In other words it may be argued that there is really no clear and precise distinction between acceptance on a theoretical level and acceptance on a practical level. In some areas of science such as atomic physics, the distinction may be particularly unclear.

For some philosophers, notably those who regard themselves as pragmatists, the notion of having two different levels of acceptance of a theory is really unnecessary.

see also...

Pragmatism

Intention

This is the mental condition in which a person plans to carry out a particular action. For instance, someone may plan to visit relatives who live a long distance away. They may find out the time of a suitable train, make arrangements to get to the station and arrive at the relatives' house. There is thus a connection between having a particular thought and fulfilling the planned action. Nevertheless, not all intentions are fulfilled. One may have the intention of becoming a film actor, but not manage to achieve this.

Intentions can refer both to fairly long-term plans and to very short-term restricted actions. For example, one may have the intention of picking up a pen from a desk. Assuming that one has the physical capability of doing this, then the intention will probably be fulfilled. Intentions may relate to physical acts such as this, which are fairly closely defined, or to bringing about future mental states which are rather more generalized. For example, one may have the intention of being more relaxed about life. However, it is less clear in this example exactly what one should do in order to bring this about. It also illustrates the problem that with such intentions it is not always clear when the intention has been fulfilled. It is much easier to know exactly when the pen has been picked up from the desk, than to know when one has achieved a more relaxed frame of mind.

There is a problem with the use of the word intention in relation to goals which may be unrealistic. The difficulty lies with deciding when something is unrealistic. For example, someone may say that they have the intention of becoming prime minister. The chances of this actually coming to pass, even if the person has all the right qualities, are fairly restricted, and we may prefer to say that this is a wish or desire, rather than an intention. The problem is that the person actually might become prime minister, just as a person who intends to become a film star may set out single-mindedly to gain acting experience, attend theatre school, and then gradually work his or her way into films. The person may be quite certain of success.

see also...

Autonomy

Jaspers, Karl

Karl Jaspers (1883–1969) was a German philosopher associated with existentialism. He was a student at the universities of Heidelberg and Berlin. The Nazi regime disapproved strongly of his writing and philosophy; yet he survived the Second World War and later became a professor at the university of Basel in Switzerland.

Jaspers had serious reservations about the limitations of the natural sciences. In his view, science could help us analyze empirical data about the world and provide a systematic account of observable phenomena. It could also help the material quality of human life through advances in technology. However, there were large areas of human existence which were not susceptible to conventional scientific enquiry, and these areas were extremely important to many human beings. Science could not help with questions about the nature of the human soul and any relationships with a transcendent being. Science could not help us with questions about the nature of existence and the purpose of life. Categories of question involving matters such as how people should use the span of human existence, and how they can explore the meaning of life and death, belonged to a different realm from that of science. In a world dominated by the approaches of science, human beings needed ways of addressing such questions about the nature of existence.

Jaspers was very interested in the nature of the 'self'. He felt that although in much of human existence, people were limited by the rather mundane cycle of events in life, they nevertheless possessed the potential to become something else. The potential of the self is in a sense limitless, and people should not feel confined by the world in which they initially find themselves. He felt that the true nature of the individual self only manifested itself during times of extreme conditions, such as considerable suffering or anguish. At such times the true qualities and potential of the self became evident.

see also...

Existentialism

Justification

The concept of justification may be used in the context of offering support for a particular action. For example, we may observe some young children playing where one child is teasing and bullying another. The second child then pushes the bully away, who falls over and bursts into tears. The second child is then worried that he or she might have used excessive force, or might get into trouble for the retaliation. In such circumstances we might say, 'Don't worry, you were justified in what you did.' The concept can thus be used to express support for a particular ethical action and to suggest, in effect, that the action concurs with the accepted norms of behaviour in society.

In another example, suppose that a doctor is treating a patient who suffers from a very complex illness. The doctor, after considerable reflection and consultation with colleagues, decides on a particular type of treatment. Unfortunately, in the light of further developments, the treatment turns out to be inappropriate and the patient's condition temporarily worsens. There is an enquiry into the matter and, having considered all of the circumstances, the enquiry panel conclude that given the evidence available at the time, the doctor's actions were justified.

The concept of justification can thus be used in relation both to ethical judgements and to epistemological issues. Generally, the use of the term raises questions about the grounds upon which we feel safe to assert that a particular course of action is warranted. Thus the fundamental questions of ethics and epistemology, and the way in which we attempt to resolve them, apply to the use of the word justify. Some philosophers take the view that there are, in principle, certain basic assumptions which do not require justification. If so, it is a separate and possibly more complex matter to establish the nature and limits of those assumptions. Other philosophers claim that there are no such basic assumptions, and that whether or not a belief can be justified rests upon, for example, the degree to which it integrates with other related beliefs.

see also...

Epistemology; Ethics

Kierkegaard, Soren

Soren Kierkegaard (1813–55) was a Danish philosopher who was very influential in the establishment of existentialism. Kierkegaard was extremely interested in the problems of existence, and what it actually means for an individual human being to feel that he or she exists. The nature of existence is seen as very unclear and uncertain, largely because there are so many choices available to individual human beings. If human beings want to truly identify the nature of their own self, then a decision must be taken in faith, to become something or somebody. The faith is needed because the decision simply to cease considering the world, and to decide to assume a particular role or function is not clear in the sense of having foreseeable outcomes. All one can do is to take a decision and believe fervently in that decision. There is inevitably an element of risk here for the individual, and it is necessary to abandon that feeling of wishing to cling on to certainty in life. Nevertheless, what is to be gained is a faith in the world and a sense for the individual of having gained a spiritual identity.

An essential feature of having identified the nature of the self is that one perceives the relationship of the individual existence to the wider world of other human beings. One begins to realize the generalized applicability of the stances one has taken. In order to reach this stage of awareness, human beings must be basically dissatisfied with their previous condition, which is characterized by uncertainties about the world. People in that condition are frequently living their lives in a manner which is, superficially at least, satisfactory but which does not possess an underlying sense of meaning. This meaning can only be obtained by making a choice about what is the most significant aspect of life for the individual and then committing to that cause. Otherwise, although a person may be fulfilling the formal conventions of life, their existence will be characterized by stress and anxiety, resulting from a lack of commitment.

see also...

Existentialism

Locke, John

John Locke (1632–1704) was an English philosopher who advocated what was fundamentally an empirical approach to philosophy. His best known publications include *Two Treatises of Government* and *Essay concerning Human Understanding*. Locke contributed to many aspects of philosophy but one of the most significant was in the area of epistemology. He did not generally subscribe to the possibility of innate knowledge, or knowledge which is somehow present in our minds from the beginning. The assumption of such a theory is that as people grow older and are educated – or perhaps simply because the environmental circumstances are advantageous – they come to a full comprehension of such 'innate' ideas. For such a theory to be possible it was felt that one had to assume that people held this potential knowledge in their own minds for a long time without realizing that it was present. This did not appear to be very likely. Rather, it appeared more probable that people's minds were totally blank from birth, and that gradually they acquired knowledge of the world by absorbing sensory data. For example, a child may learn that teasing the family dog brings a rebuke from parents and, if the behaviour persists, then parents become very angry. On one level the child simply learns that behaviour X results in response Y. However, the next stage in acquiring knowledge is that people reflect upon the world and upon the sense data they have received, and generate new knowledge based upon those reflections. The child, for example, may tease the cat and elicit the same reproach from parents. At this stage, the child may relate the two experiences and form a judgement about the ethics of teasing family pets, or even animals in general.

Locke has been criticized on the basis that once people have considered and evaluated sense data, they may form different conclusions about it. The conclusion of person A may be different from the conclusion of person B. It may be rather difficult to know who is correct and, even more so, whether either conclusion reflects something existing in the empirical world.

see also...

Empiricism

Logical Positivism

This was a philosophical movement which saw the purpose of philosophy to be to clarify the nature of statements about the world, and also to indicate how one might set about judging their truth or falsity. Until the advent of logical positivism, grand theories of philosophy had generally sought to provide knowledge of the human condition, the universe and of ethical principles. Logical positivism rejected such grand designs for philosophy and claimed that its only real purpose was to some extent more limited.

Logical positivists argued that the statements we make about the world can be divided into two broad categories. Analytic statements are those which present the subject matter of the sentence in a slightly different way, without adding any more information. For example, the statement 'The rain is wet' does not add anything to our knowledge of rain. We know rain is wet, because wetness is part of the notion of rain. On the other hand, the statement 'The rain is warm' is of a different type. Rain does not have to be warm. We would have to feel it on the skin to know how it felt. Such statements are known as synthetic statements.

Logical positivists argued that the function of philosophy was to divide statements into the analytic and the synthetic. The former would be true because of their form and the latter could be tested by gathering empirical data. Positivists considered all other statements to be lacking in any sense. The main function of philosophy then, is considered to be not the creation of new knowledge, but rather to show people the type of data which would be needed to demonstrate either the truth of a statement, or that the statement was false. Logical positivism is associated historically with the 'Vienna Circle' of philosophers, including Moritz Schlick and Rudolf Carnap, which met in the two decades before the Second World War. Among English philosophers, Alfred Ayer (1910–89) is regarded as perhaps the main advocate of logical positivism and is well known for his book *Language, Truth and Logic*.

see also...

Analytic Proposition; Empiricism

58

Marx, Karl

Karl Marx (1818–83) was a German philosopher and political thinker, whose writings ranged across a number of fields including economics and history. He was born in Trier and studied at the universities of Bonn and Berlin. He wrote for the radical newspaper the *Rheinische Zeitung*, but eventually left Germany and went to live first in Paris, and later London. Much of Marx's writings involved an analysis of the capitalist system, using in considerable part underlying concepts derived from Hegel. Marx argued that there were two main classes in society, the capitalists who owned and monopolized the factories and industrial production, and the large numbers of workers who laboured in those factories; maximizing profits for, and working ultimately for the benefit of the capitalists. Marx argued that such a system was deeply unfair and that eventually the workers would recognize these profound inequalities and would become conscious of their own social class position. This imbalance would in turn result in an instability in the economic and political system, and the working class would assume power and control of the productive system. This would simultaneously result in a fairer society – a communist society.

The theories of Marx consist of a variety of economic, historical, philosophical and political ideas combined into a wide-ranging analysis. There is, however, a strong ethical trend in Marx's writings, particularly about the nature of human beings in a capitalist society. The capitalist system has the effect of alienating workers because they begin to see the exploitative nature of the society in which they are working. The industrial system has the potential to make the lives of ordinary people much easier, and yet under capitalism the effects are simply to use people as a source of labour to increase the profits of the factory owners. Marx argued that a socialist society would eliminate this sense of alienation and result in a more equitable system. However, Marx has been criticized in that of late capitalism has appeared relatively successful.

see also...
Dialectic

Materialism

This is the view that everything in the world can be explained on a material or physical plane, and hence that there is no need to consider or hypothesize the mind or mental events. As with most philosophical positions there are various degrees to which philosophers may subscribe to a materialist view. Some may entirely reject the notion of mind, of thought, or of mental activity, with the only significant aspect of the world being on the physical plane. On the other hand, materialists may accept the impact of mind and thought, but explain them on a purely physical level as consisting of electrical impulses across synapses and in neurones. The mind, on this model, simply becomes a special case of the material world.

Much of the position advocated by materialists depends upon the particular concept of mind which they are using. It is very difficult to imagine a condition in which the entire nature of existence is material because, if that were the case, there would be no mind to appreciate and understand the physical world. Besides, there are some kinds of conscious activities which are difficult to equate to physical objects. For example, thoughts themselves seem to be of a very different nature from physical objects. They cannot be touched, they cannot be seen, and they do not occupy physical space. Equally, there are some kinds of apparently mental activity which are difficult to equate with a purely physical world. For example, religious and mystical inclinations, or love of music and works of art, do not seem to operate on a purely materialist level. It is rather difficult, then, to sustain the view that the world operates exclusively on a material level. It seems reasonable to hypothesize some kind of mental activity.

Materialism or materialistic are terms also used on a purely populist level to refer to people who attach a lot of importance to consumer goods. The only significance for philosophy here, is that it does raise ethical issues.

see also...

Philosophy of Religion

Mean, The

This is a theory of ethics deriving from the work of the Greek philosopher Aristotle (384–322 BCE). Aristotle was a student of Plato at the Academy in Athens. On Plato's death Aristotle left, ultimately working in Macedonia as tutor to the future Alexander the Great. Aristotle eventually returned to Athens and founded his own school called the Lyceum. In terms of ethics, Aristotle's view was that it is reasonable for human beings to pursue happiness but that the latter is not achieved by living a life of excess. For example, suppose a person loves foreign travel. The argument would be that if such a person travelled continuously he or she might begin to find it difficult to appreciate the places visited and the excitement of travel might wane. On the other hand, if such a person rarely had the opportunity to travel, then this would not enhance his or her happiness. Aristotle's argument would be that ideally there should be the opportunity for sufficient travel to maintain the excitement of the experience, but not an excess such that the excitement disappears. In other words, one should aim for the mean and have a reasonable amount of travel.

Now Aristotle did not suggest that everyone should have exactly the same amount of travel, or of food, drink, exercise, social interaction or anything else. His proposition was that the 'mean' did not signify an arithmetic mean but rather a moderate amount of the variable concerned, which would be most likely to engender happiness in the person concerned. This moderate amount of the particular variable would be different for different individuals. In addition, each person would establish only what was appropriate for him or her by a process of investigation. There was, according to Aristotle, no fixed amount of anything which was appropriate for all people. Aristotle's idea of the mean was first relativistic in the sense that the mean for one person might be different from that for another person; and second that it should be based upon experimental investigation.

see also...
Ethics

Meaning

Meaning is what people understand a word or sentence to signify in a public language. If I asked a group of people what they meant by a book, they would probably describe an object with a large number of printed pages bound together permanently. If I asked them whether an object with one page, ten pages, or twenty pages could count as a book, they might reject this and say that such an object is a pamphlet. If, on the other hand, I described three hundred pages held together in a ring binder, they might say this is not a book, but a file or manuscript. In other words, people are generally able to appreciate the meaning of a word and to describe the limits of the publicly acceptable usage of the term. This has led to the suggestion that the meaning of a word is the picture which it conjures up in the mind. So perhaps 'book' conjures up a picture of rows of similar objects on the shelves of a library. We could also regard this as the literal meaning of the word 'book.'

It may appear that meaning can be thought of most clearly as the range of things to which a word refers in the public arena. Thus a dog refers to a four-footed furry animal which barks. On this understanding of meaning, we can connect a word with an object in the real world. The word 'refers' to an object, and this is sometimes termed the referential theory of meaning. We can also employ this theory of meaning to abstract nouns such as 'happiness', since we can refer both to internal psychological states associated with happiness, and also the external appearance of people who claim to be happy. However, the theory does not really help us to understand the meaning of the word Martian since we cannot refer to examples of Martians in the currently known external world.

It has been argued that meaning is essentially a matter of social definition. Within this framework, the meaning of terms is seen as being negotiated by different social groups. For example, a group of people trying to gain political change in a society may be seen as freedom fighters by some, or as terrorists by others.

see also...

Essentialism

62

Merleau-Ponty, Maurice

Maurice Merleau-Ponty (1907–1961) was a French philosopher very much associated with existentialism and phenomenology. In the 1920s he was a student at the Ecole Normale Superieure at the same time as Jean-Paul Sartre. He held professorships at both the Sorbonne and at the College de France. His books include *Phenomenology of Perception, The Structure of Behaviour* and *The Visible and the Invisible.*

Merleau-Ponty was rather doubtful about the methods and goals of orthodox philosophy and particularly of the analytic approach to philosophy. He felt rather that the latter attempted to generate final, conclusive answers to the great questions of philosophy, whereas he felt that this was a very difficult goal to achieve. In particular, he advocated a method of critical reflection to replace analysis in philosophy. Reflection would not have the disadvantage of tending to disaggregate philosophical problems to a stage where one was in danger of losing sight of the totality of the issue.

He also became very well known for addressing some of the philosophical questions deriving from the position of the human body in relation to philosophical problems. For example, the body had been viewed by a number of philosophers as an object in the world, considered and reflected upon by a separate mind. Merleau-Ponty argued very strongly that the body was more 'subject' than 'object', and was an integral part of understanding the position of a human individual in the world. He suggested that traditionally there had been two principal methods of comprehending the world. First, there had been the method of *a priori* analysis and second, the process of analyzing empirical data. He argued that there should be more of an emphasis upon the kind of direct experience of the world which takes place before we start to think about and analyze our experiences. For example, if we are walking along a cliff top beside the ocean, we have direct experiences of our surroundings which, within this perspective, provide a valid understanding of the world.

see also...

Existentialism; Phenomenology

Metaphysics

This is a branch of philosophy which deals with fundamental problems of the universe, such as whether or not there is a distinction between what we call 'mind' and what we call 'matter'. The origin of the term dates back to a summary of the writings of Aristotle, where the section dealing with such questions was placed after that on physics, giving rise to the term meta-physics (beyond-physics). There is increasingly a debate about the limitations of metaphysics and whether there are actually any legitimately metaphysical questions.

Metaphysics purports to deal with what exists, as opposed to epistemology which is concerned with the grounds on which we know that things exist. Many questions can be identified as being scientific in nature and hence not the subject of metaphysics. If a question can be resolved by the analysis of empirical data, then it is not normally metaphysical. In addition, if an issue is essentially mathematical, then it is not normally metaphysical. Any other questions may be purportedly metaphysical.

In the example above, if mind and matter are essentially different, then the explanation of that difference becomes a metaphysical question. On the other hand, some neuro-physiologists might claim that the functions of the mind can be simply reduced to a complex series of biochemical reactions, and that the mind and the physical world are essentially identical in nature.

Although perhaps we can conceive the possibility that such a question can be reduced to an empirical level, it may be a little harder to achieve with other issues. For example, some may argue that the universe is directed either by a spiritual force or, at least, in the sense that it appears to be developing in a particular way. On the other hand, others may suggest that the universe is essentially random in nature and that its fundamental feature is its unpredictability.

see also...

Ontology

Mill, John Stuart

John Stuart Mill (1806–73) was a British philosopher well known for his comments on social issues and for his publication *On Liberty* (1860). He wrote for the journal, the *Westminster Review*, worked for the East India Company, and was a Member of Parliament.

In broad ethical terms, Mill subscribed to the principles of utilitarianism, arguing that actions were right if they contributed to the creation of better living conditions for the majority of people. He extended this type of argument to a consideration of a much broader range of social issues and felt that social and political institutions should be judged by the criteria of whether they enhanced the human condition. He implied that some institutions could easily lose touch with their true function of improving the quality of life of individual people. In particular, although he felt that the capitalist system brought many advantages, he was also conscious that the system entailed the labour of large numbers of ordinary people who were not necessarily as advantaged by the system as were the owners of capital. He considered that under some circumstances a system which involved the shared ownership of capital could be more fair and equitable. Mill was a great advocate of individual liberty and considered that both governments and institutions could act (if sometimes inadvertently) in ways which reduced liberty. He therefore felt that measures should be taken wherever possible to provide safeguards for human freedom.

In a not unconnected argument, he espoused the right of women to have the vote and argued strongly for the equality of treatment of women in society. In particular, he felt that women should have equal rights in terms of educational opportunities. The provision of equality for women would, he felt, enhance the position of both men and women, and generally improve the way both genders related to each other.

see also...

Feminism; Utilitarianism

Naturalism

This is the view that all aspects of human existence and of the world in general can be explained in terms of naturally existing or observable phenomena. For example, Darwin's explanation of evolution, employing as it does the process of natural selection, is a naturalistic explanation. Within Darwin's view, evolution does not require any theological or metaphysical explanation. One can understand the process on the basis of both observation and verifiable scientific principles.

In terms of human behaviour, a naturalistic explanation would be one which employs generalizable statements derived from psychological observation or, taking the issue one step further, one which is based on biochemical reactions at a cellular level. In ethics, a naturalistic theory is one which claims that it is possible to ascertain whether an act is ethically right or wrong by analysis of the empirically observable features of the theory or the act. For example, utilitarianism is a naturalistic theory when it advocates the greatest happiness of the greatest number, since systematic observation would be required in order to estimate the extent of the happiness generated.

The Cambridge philosopher, George Edward Moore (1873–1958) was well known for arguing that naturalism cannot be used as the basis for moral judgements. He argued that we cannot logically define a 'good' deed in terms of scientific or empirical description. For example, suppose a person argues that we ought to exercise every day because exercise improves the blood circulation. We probably would not dispute that generally speaking exercise does improve the circulation, and in many individuals improves the health. However, the injunction to exercise every day begs the question about exactly how much exercise is required, and whether the same amount and type of exercise is needed by everyone. Whereas many people would agree that exercise assists the process of being healthy, it is a separate matter whether we have a moral obligation to exercise.

see also...

Empiricism; Ethics; Utilitarianism

Necessary Condition

This is a logical way of looking at the relationship between two events, or at the way in which one situation can affect another. As with many concepts in philosophy, it is much easier to consider a practical situation. If we think, for example, of an electric table lamp, then it is a necessary condition for the bulb to light, that electricity be flowing through the bulb. If there is no electricity flowing, then the bulb simply will not light. Electricity is necessary for that type of lamp to light. It is important to remember, however, that there may be other conditions which must prevail to ensure that the bulb will light. Even if the lamp is connected to the electric socket, the bulb will not light if the filament is broken. There may be a whole range of necessary conditions which must be operable.

Thus, logically we can argue that if the lamp is lit, there must be electricity; but we cannot say that if there is electricity, then it will light. Equally well, if the lamp is not lit, we cannot logically argue that this is because of an absence of electricity. There may be other factors which are preventing the electricity from flowing properly and hence causing light. It is also true that the presence of electricity does not always result in light. Depending upon the nature of the conducting wire and on the size of the electric current flowing, heat energy may be produced, but no light energy.

The idea of a necessary condition should not be thought of as being the same as a 'cause'. For example, we might consider the presence of water to be a necessary condition for a plant to grow, but we would be unlikely to think of water as the 'cause' of the plant growing. The idea of the cause of an event, or of trying to establish a causal connection between two events, is a complex activity. The notion of a necessary condition is helpful to analyze the nature of the background circumstances which must be present before an event can occur. These examples may seem rather straightforward but, in a more complex situation, the idea of a necessary condition is a useful analytic tool.

see also...
Sufficient Condition

Non-violence

This is primarily an ethical doctrine that one should avoid aggressive and damaging acts against other living things. Within this broad moral imperative there are a number of significant variations depending upon the particular concept of violence which is held, and upon the circumstances which one might feel could create an exception to the general rule. Some people may argue that the principle of non-violence should apply only to animals, and not to plants. Others may wish to argue that the thoughtless picking of wild flowers or snapping of twigs from a tree, are essentially acts of violence to be avoided. In the latter sense, non-violence is very much akin to the principle of treating the environment with care and sensitivity.

Non-violence can also be thought of as applying to the psychological context as well as the physical. In this sense, it can be argued that non-violence involves restraining oneself from having angry or vengeful thoughts against a person. However, most people would associate non-violence with the strategy of non-retaliation when threatened, and not returning violence with more violence.

The principle of non-violence has also been used, not only as an ethical principle but also as a specific strategy, to support a political struggle. It was especially noteworthy for its use by Mahatma Gandhi; first in his struggle in South Africa to support the rights of Indian migrant workers, and later in the struggle against the British for Indian independence. Gandhi always argued that no matter what the provocation during a political struggle, the use of violence undermined the case that was being made. His supporters were frequently the subject of violent attacks, but Gandhi always urged them to submit peacefully to this violence, while at the same time making clear their case.

The philosophical doctrine as well as its use as a political strategy has, since Gandhi's time, been taken up by a large number of campaigning groups.

see also...

Philosophy of Religion

Objectivism

This is the contention in ethics that there are certain moral principles which are true and which are quite independent of the beliefs of individual human beings. For example, it may be argued that the deliberate taking of human life is always morally wrong, however extreme the situation. A soldier may argue that if he discovers one of his comrades mortally wounded and in great pain, begging him to put an end to his misery, that the ethically correct course of action would be to comply with his wishes. However, the ethical objectivist would argue that this is wrong, on the grounds of the supposed objectivity of the principle of not taking life.

It is a matter of reasonable debate how objective moral principles can be known. Some argue that they can be realized by observation of the empirical world. For example, it could be argued that the proposed moral principle 'lying is wrong' can be developed out of observations of the chaos resulting when people start to lie habitually. When we become uncertain whether people are telling the truth or not, the cohesion of human relationships starts to break down. Others argue that some objective principles are so much a part of what it means to be human, that they can be derived without the need for empirical evidence. For example, one might suggest that the principle 'it is wrong to wilfully cause pain to another' falls into this category.

One of the strengths of objectivism in ethics is that it enables us to reach clear decisions for action, and indeed many people look to philosophers to provide this kind of guidance. Objectivism allows a comparison to be made between different options. However, those who argue against objectivism do so on the grounds that it is apparently difficult to know the objectively correct course of action. When a dispute develops, the opponents of objectivism say that it is not easy to appreciate the kind of evidence which might be adduced to settle the argument.

---

see also...

Ethics; Subjectivism

Ontology

This is the branch of philosophy which is concerned with what we believe does or does not exist. We can apply the term to a particular world view, perspective or theory. Each of the latter will almost certainly have a number of concepts representing things which are assumed to exist within that particular world view. We can speak of the ontology of that world view as being the sum total of the associated ideas which are assumed to represent reality. The existence of God, for example, is part of a theological perspective on the world and on existence.

As one might anticipate, philosophers differ quite widely in their views concerning what does or does not exist. For example, if philosopher A believes in the idea of goodness as being a quality which is real and tangible, philosopher B may wish to argue that goodness is not at all real. Philosopher B may suggest that if an action is thought of as good, then it is simple to say that one approves of it. Philosopher B may accuse A of reification, or trying to make real something which is not real.

The debate about whether or not things are real is a long-standing issue, and philosophers may be divided very broadly into two camps. Realists argue that we should seek reality in the world external to human minds, whereas idealists suggest that if you wish to identify reality you should do so within one's own or other people's minds.

As an example, we could take the idea of 'social class'. Realists would argue that class exists as a living, functioning reality of society. People understand the social class they belong to and associate themselves with that social class. Idealists would perhaps argue that class is a mental construct, designed to help us make sense of society, but not necessarily mirrored or replicated in the real world.

see also...

Epistemology; Idealism

Pantheism

This is a view of the universe and of God which suggests that God is the same as all living and inanimate objects in the universe. It is not so much that pantheists see God as a part of all things, as if there were a spark of divinity in everything, but rather that everything in the universe is a part of God. Versions of pantheism assume, for example, that there is a divine spirit throughout the universe which is part of the divine spirit of God.

Many theistic religious systems tend to assume that there is an all-powerful external God who controls the universe and provides guidance on how human beings should conduct their lives. This conceptualization of God is not really relevant to pantheism. If all living things are part of the divine, it carries a number of implications for human conduct. The way in which human beings treat the environment and plants, for example, must be affected by a view which sees plants as being part of God. Equally well, if we mistreat a fellow human being, then we also mistreat God.

Moreover, we cannot rely any more on a set of moral precepts determined by or derived from God, because God does not exist as a separate entity from us. Rather, we must construct our own moral and religious precepts, deriving them first from principles, and applying them as our conscience dictates. With pantheism, however, there are likely to be differences of opinion between people as to how we should derive religious precepts. Pantheism casts much more responsibility upon the individual to develop his or her perception of the world.

Perhaps the most famous advocate of pantheism was the Dutch philosopher Baruch Spinoza (1632–77). He saw God and the natural world as being the same and derived much of his ethical views from his basic idea of the nature of God. As it was not possible to have precise guidance from God in terms of ethical precepts, Spinoza suggested that each individual should attempt to analyze how God would want them to behave and act.

see also...
Philosophy of Religion

Paradigm

When we think about the world we do so from a particular viewpoint, using a range of ideas and concepts. At certain times in history, specific ways of thinking about the world have predominated. Each particular world view can be termed a paradigm. Different paradigms may co-exist and overlap. At the moment, perhaps the predominant paradigm is that of science. Most people may not think of themselves as operating within a scientific paradigm, and yet arguably they do. The scientific paradigm is characterized by a logical and rational style of argument; by testing suggestions and hypotheses using data; by tending to emphasize empirical methods rather than, say, intuition; and by trying to develop general statements or theories in order to explain events. Many television adverts, for example, try to market products by using a scientific paradigm. A new toothpaste is shown being used in a series of tests to determine whether it reduces tooth decay; new motor car tyres are shown in experiments designed to test their stopping distance; and household cleaners are shown being used in tests to compare their cleaning properties or the degree to which they eliminate bacteria. The assumption behind this approach is that television viewers will accept the general arguments that scientific tests of this kind are reliable demonstrations of the worth of the products. Equally, if we have a plumbing or electrical fault in our home, we expect the tradesperson to identify the fault, to seek evidence for the cause of the problem, to attempt to rectify it, and finally to test whether the original malfunction has been remedied. This belief in the logical, rational scientific method is widespread.

A well-known philosopher of science, Thomas Kuhn, has argued that throughout history one paradigm has replaced another, as the original one proved incapable of explaining the current view of the world. For example, in medieval Europe a cosmology founded upon the Earth at the centre of the universe was replaced by a cosmology which placed the sun at the centre of the solar system.

see also...

Philosophy of Science

Phenomenology

Phenomenology is a technique for examining the social world and trying to understand it. The approach was first developed by the German philosopher Edmund Husserl (1859–1938). Phenomenology has become rather a diverse philosophical approach but its key philosophical ideas are as follows. Phenomenology does not rely exclusively upon empirical data. While not disregarding data which has been collected through the senses, it places just as much emphasis upon thought processes. If we are thinking about something, reflecting upon it, analyzing it or comparing it in our minds, then the results of this thought process are just as much to be regarded as 'data', as if we collected data in a laboratory experiment. Related to this is the phenomenological idea that the object which is being observed or heard, exists as a continuity with the mental process by which it is observed or heard. In other words, it is difficult or indeed impossible to separate the act of observation from that which is observed. Inevitably a mental process must take place which seeks to understand and interpret the object of observation.

This mental process may be subtly different for each observer, giving rise to the view that there is a certain subjectivity in phenomenological research.

It is central to the phenomenological approach that our understanding of the world depends as much, or even more, on mental intuition and insights, than on sense data. In other words, the way in which a human being thinks about and analyzes the world is critical in forming a personal understanding of it. As an example, let us suppose that someone has a deep-seated affection for nature and the natural world. The person has no remembrance of when this affinity started, nor whether it was based on any particular external event. All the person knows is that he or she feels a profound sense of peace when in remote, natural environments. Now phenomenologists would argue that these feelings and sense of well-being are just as much data as the empirical data of the scientist.

see also...

Philosophy of the Social Sciences

Philosophy of Education

This is generally conceived as the application of philosophical analysis to the contemporary concepts of education. The process seeks partly to demonstrate that many of the concepts of education are far from straightforward. In so doing, philosophy of education draws upon all of the major branches of philosophy.

Much attention has been given to epistemological questions relating to the curriculum. The issue of the subjects which young people study is important as it affects the knowledge which future generations will possess. One of the key philosophical questions is whether some subjects are fundamentally more important than others, and hence should be selected for passing on to future generations. If we accept this distinction between subjects, then philosophers are interested in the criteria which we might use. The issue of a national curriculum across a society is an important matter for philosophers because it raises questions about the range of knowledge and skills to which school students ought to be exposed, and also about the aims of education. The latter issue leads us to consider the qualities which an education system is presumably trying to inculcate in its future citizens.

The notion of a centrally administered curriculum raises questions about the process by which knowledge is to be transmitted and also about the underpinning value system of the curriculum. Here we are in the realm of ethics. The notion of an implicit or explicit value system also suggests a potential relationship with notions of ideology. Should the curriculum be value-neutral, or should it avowedly espouse certain principles and values. If the latter, then philosophers would be very interested to analyze the processes by which certain values are selected.

Philosophers of education have also carried out a considerable amount of work in trying to distinguish between education as a concept, and related concepts such as training. In this way, they have sought to establish some of the key features of education as a process.

see also...
Dewey, John; Epistemology; Ethics

Philosophy of Religion

This involves the application of philosophical analysis to the concepts and ideas which are characteristic of religion. Many aspects of religion are sociological in nature, for example, issues about the power exercised by organized religions. Other features are psychological, for example, in terms of the cognitive attitudes which might tend to encourage someone to join a particular religious group. Other religious ideas do however raise philosophical questions. The nature of religious knowledge is a fundamental issue in the philosophy of religion. Suppose that a religious teacher or leader suggests that we should act in a certain way and that only this certain way is likely to lead to salvation. We would be left with two immediate philosophical questions. How do we know that the leader is right in advocating a certain behaviour? What is the nature of the condition described as salvation?

Much of the analysis of religious knowledge has centred on the supposed difference between natural and revealed religious experience. A natural religious experience is one which develops from a natural experience, such as the feeling of peace or well-being that might result from a long walk in the country. One might feel a sense of unity with nature; with the stream of life. One might have a sense of being part of the natural progression of things and that the universe is being directed by an external power. Even if one does not conceptualize this as involving God, then it is still arguably a religious experience. Revealed religious knowledge on the other hand derives from the particular insights of a religious teacher or mystic. Sometimes such a person is part of a long religious tradition, such as Buddhism, where there is a clearly established body of received wisdom, and the teacher interprets it to the adherents of that tradition. In other cases, an individual teacher may teach a new tradition and set of precepts.

In the case of both natural and revealed religion, one wants to establish the status of the experiences which people claim to have had.

see also...

Atheism

Philosophy of Science

The philosophy of science covers a range of important questions such as the nature of science itself; the kind of knowledge which scientific enquiry can reveal; the processes of scientific research and their characteristics; the differences (if any) between research processes in the natural sciences and in the social sciences; and the use and meaning of concepts such as law, theory and hypothesis.

A fundamental question in the philosophy of science is whether there is a basic approach to the establishment of new knowledge which is common to all empirical subject areas. For example, one might ask whether empirical enquiry and scientific enquiry are describing the same activities. To put it another way, can research in history, English literature, sociology, or psychology be described as scientific? This raises the fundamental philosophical question of how to define 'science'.

Perhaps science can best be seen as a process, with certain broad characteristics. It is usually assumed that it entails the establishment of a hypothesis which is a provisional statement about the world, which the researcher seeks to test. Data is then gathered and analyzed in an attempt to either confirm the hypothesis or to demonstrate that it cannot be supported. It has been suggested that even if a hypothesis is apparently supported, then the search should continue for data which does not support it. Science is thus always seen as generating provisional results. We never arrive at a situation where we can say something with absolute certainty. There seems no reason in principle why this general type of process could not be used in a wide variety of subject areas, with at least some of the research problems therein. Nevertheless, there are doubts whether it is possible to delineate precisely a single scientific method which can be used in all contexts. There are differences in the approach to knowledge in different subjects. Moreover, one can make out the case that all scientific enquiry takes place within a framework of social and cultural values.

see also...

Popper, Karl R.

Philosophy of the Social Sciences

This discipline involves the philosophical issues raised by the study of society. Considerable attention is often devoted to the epistemological and ontological issues raised by the nature of sociological knowledge. For example, one of the traditional ways of investigating society has been to employ the approaches of the natural scientists. Sociologists have attempted to measure social class, and psychologists measure intelligence, using the same philosophical approach as a physicist measuring electrical conductivity. In other words, social class and intelligence are treated as if they are specific measurable entities.

More recent developments in social science have tended to view such concepts as socially constructed. In other words, the individual members of society interact and, through the everyday use of words and ideas, a shared understanding of a concept gradually evolves. Knowledge tends therefore, not to be seen as 'given' or defined externally, but to be created and re-created through the social interaction of individuals. These two views about the nature of social

knowledge give rise to very different approaches to the study of society. Broadly speaking, the former leads to the use of quantitative methods and the latter qualitative methods.

The methods of the natural sciences have tended to apply the process of hypothesis testing to social science, and also to seek to analyze clear relationships between variables, leading to the possibility of establishing causal relationships. The fundamental problem here is that of the very large number of variables operating in social environments and the difficulty of eliminating some of these from the research. Such investigations have also sought to generalize from the research, and to explore ways in which the conclusions can be applied to other contexts. Interpretive research, on the other hand, using largely qualitative methods has given priority to seeking to understand small-scale social interaction.

see also...

Critical Theory; Feminism; Functionalism; Phenomenology

Plato

Plato (*c.*427–347 BCE) is probably one of the best-known philosophers. He was born in Athens into a very wealthy family and as a young man was a student of Socrates. When the latter died in 399 BCE, Plato embarked on a period of extensive travel, returning to Athens some years later. In 387 BCE he established the Academy – a school devoted to philosophical debate and learning. Aristotle was a student at the Academy for about the last twenty years of Plato's life.

Perhaps the most famous of Plato's writings are the Dialogues, some of which present the arguments advocated by Socrates, and others which add Plato's own thoughts. Plato frequently illustrates what may be termed the Socratic Method of teaching, whereby the teacher leads the student to a better understanding of an issue, by means of a systematic question and answer technique. This method tends to assume that the learner has the potential understanding and knowledge within them, but needs to be brought to a full comprehension of it through the careful questioning of the teacher. Plato is particularly well known for his Theory of Forms. This theory suggests that there exists an abstract and eternal notion of concepts such as 'goodness'. Within this theory it is assumed that particular examples of, say, good behaviour, are simply individual instances of the form of the good.

Plato was also very much concerned with political philosophy. He was interested in the characteristics of what might be termed the perfect state or society. He saw this as being a society characterized by rationality and justice, and only a 'philosopher-king' who ruled with objectivity and disinterest could engender this type of state. Plato suggested that one could be trained philosophically in order to appreciate the nature of goodness and morality and, henceforth, such people would behave in an ethical way and potentially be capable of acting as wise and just rulers. It was an assumption of Plato's ethics that goodness was not a relative concept.

see also...

Idealism

Political Philosophy

This is the study of the systems whereby an individual relates to the state and to federations of states. It also includes the relationship between individuals and the large organizations which make up the governmental processes of the state. Usually such organizations and the state provide a range of services to the individual citizen, while at the same time exerting varying degrees of control over individuals. The important concepts of political philosophy are concerned with the manner in which this fundamental relationship between the individual and the state is managed.

An important group of concepts in political philosophy include autonomy, freedom and liberty. In any state, the individual will seek certain rights, such as the right of self-expression and freedom of speech, and the right to comment publicly upon the nature of government. The degree to which the state permits these freedoms will depend upon the state's view of such concepts as justice, authority, power and political tolerance. In principle, states run on socialist lines may permit a certain number of such freedoms, whereas totalitarian or authoritarian states may permit very few liberties.

A central aspect of political philosophy is the manner and degree to which the state's resources are distributed equitably among its citizens. To some extent these issues are economic and can be included in the area of political economy. An important issue is the extent to which the state allows a free market to operate, with the possible result that some sections of society may have limited access to rewarding employment, a healthy lifestyle and adequate life chances. The alternative is to centrally control the selective distribution of wealth to try to ensure some degree of equality in access to resources for individual citizens. The varying degree to which a government seeks to achieve this is a reflection of its political ideology. The latter term encompasses the sets of values and the general world view of a government or administration.

see also...

Democracy; Hobbes, Thomas; Marx, Karl; Plato

Popper, Karl R.

ir Karl Popper (1902–94) was born in Austria and completed his doctorate at the University of Vienna. For a major part of his career he held a professorship at the London School of Economics. His main writings have been in the area of the philosophy of scientific method and in the philosophy of the social sciences.

Popper argued that one of the main characteristics of science was that one should try to disprove, or falsify, a theory. He suggested that traditionally there had been a tendency to always seek data which supported a theory, and hence to try to give the theory even more credibility. He argued that this general approach was less than rigorous from a scientific point of view. The more rigorous approach was to try to find falsifying data. If such falsifying data could not be found then the theory remained provisionally accepted and one was entitled to assume it was acceptable for practical purposes. Nevertheless, in principle, the search for contrary evidence should never cease. If, on the other hand, it was possible to identify some falsifying data, then either the theory should be totally discarded or at least amended to fit the new evidence. Having established the revised theory, the search for falsifying data should then be resumed. In other words, scientific theory is continually regarded as provisional, subject always to the identification of falsifying data.

In relation to his social philosophy, Popper advocated what he described as an 'open society' as being the most favourable form of social organization. This was characterised by the freedom of individual citizens to voice their concerns about the structure and organization of society, and indeed for there to be systems in place for the leaders of society to be replaced by others through peaceful processes. Popper was distrustful of large scale social planning which could possibly reflect the interests and values of small groups of people. He advocated smaller-scale change to seek continually to amend undesirable trends in society.

see also...

Democracy; Political Philosophy

Positivism

This is a particular approach to the study of the social sciences developed by the French philosopher and sociologist Auguste Comte (1798–1857). It characteristically proposes the methodology of the natural sciences for investigating the social sciences. For example, if someone was investigating the attitudes of people from different sectors of society to watching television, then using positivistic methods they might count the number of people who watched a particular programme, or count the number of programmes of different types watched by specific social groups. The emphasis would be upon using broadly quantitative methods and setting up hypotheses for future testing. Once the data had been analyzed there would characteristically be attempts to generalize from the data, so that any results could be applied in different contexts.

Critics of positivism argue that it provides a very limited and superficial picture of the social world. What is interesting in the above example, they would argue, is not so much how many programmes people watch, but why they watch the programmes they do. Here, they argue, the research approaches of physics and chemistry are not really going to work. Positivism may provide for the researcher a description of social events, and may also outline some possible causal connections, but it cannot, so its critics argue, provide an account of the underlying mechanisms of social behaviour.

In its favour, positivism has been very useful in providing a picture of very broad macro trends in society, particularly using quantitative research methods. These large-scale patterns can then be used to generate more in-depth questions, which are not as susceptible to quantitative approaches and require more qualitative methods. The debate concerning the relative advantages and disadvantages of positivistic methods on the one hand, and interpretive methods on the other, is one of the central questions of the philosophy of the social sciences.

see also...

Logical Positivism

Pragmatism

This is a practically oriented approach to philosophy which developed in the United States in the nineteenth century. It is associated with, among others, Charles Sanders Peirce (1839–1914), William James (1842–1910) and John Dewey (1859–1952). Although receiving a slightly different emphasis in different writers, the essence of pragmatism is that it is not sufficient to assert something is true unless that truth also works in practical situations. For example, psychologists seek to distinguish between intrinsic motivation and extrinsic motivation. These are respectively the idea that individuals are driven by an internal impetus such as ambition or a desire to learn, or alternatively that they are driven by external forces such as a need for money or a fear of punishment. Now a pragmatist would argue that such a distinction may or may not be true and that the way to establish the validity of the distinction is to establish whether the two concepts are practically useful in explaining different examples of human behaviour. If they are not useful in this regard, then this undermines the extent to which they can be regarded as valid.

Apart from epistemological questions, pragmatists would also apply the same criteria to ethical theories. According to pragmatists an ethical theory should be judged purely on the extent to which it helps to resolve practical dilemmas or act as a guide or set of criteria by which individuals can solve their own moral problems. The difficulty with practical utility as an exclusive criterion to judge philosophical theories, is that circumstances change. A theory may function well in one context and yet be inapplicable in another. An ethical theory may provide an apparently straightforward resolution of one question, yet under different circumstances it may be very difficult to apply.

An argument in support of pragmatism is that ideas clearly do have practical application and indeed do influence practical events. One has only to think of politics where the ideas of politicians, often based upon theoretical positions, are translated into practical policies.

see also...

Dewey, John

Rationalism

This is the approach to knowledge which assumes that it is possible to reach absolute certainty about the world, purely by mental processes. One form of rationalism suggests that human beings are born with certain innate ideas which are entirely unaffected by our everyday experience. On the other hand, another version suggests that while we do learn by observing the world around us, our essential knowledge of the world is gained by mental reflection and thought.

One of the basic difficulties with an epistemology which is rationalistic, is that it is difficult to compare different claims to truth. If one person claims that X is a fair way to behave, while another says Y is the only fair way, it is not easy to know how to resolve the matter. We could take a poll and ask a large number of individuals whether they feel X or Y is the most fair. This would not however resolve the rationalistic claims to fairness; it would merely tell us what a large number of people thought. Alternatively, we could test out X and Y and observe the consequences of employing them.

The problem here would be that some people may feel that the consequences of X are desirable and yet others would disagree. The same would probably be true of Y. It is not always easy to evaluate the consequences of actions anyway. We can often see both good and bad features in human situations. Indeed, the history of ideas suggests that philosophers and thinkers have rarely agreed on rationalistic theories of knowledge. Critics of rationalism have hence suggested that all we are really considering are the personal intuitions of individual philosophers. Empiricists, who emphasize the importance of everyday experience in constructing a theory of knowledge, argue that they can collect evidence to support or challenge their theories, while there is no systematic way of investigating the claims of rationalists. Historically, rationalism is associated with the Greek philosopher Plato and the French philosopher Rene Descartes.

---

see also...

Descartes, Rene; Empiricism; Plato

Relativism

Teachers can sometimes be heard saying to their pupils, 'You cannot just do as you like; this school has certain standards.' Alternatively, they might say, 'You cannot behave like that here; we have a particular way of doing things.' Philosophically speaking, the teachers who say such things are arguing against a kind of relativism. They are saying that they do not want a school community where one pupil's view of behaviour is just as good as that of another, no matter how eccentric or antisocial they may be. They are arguing for certain standards of behaviour which are implicitly 'correct' and which should be adopted by all members of the school.

We may feel that this is a reasonable point of view. Surely we cannot have a free-for-all when it comes to pupil behaviour? If this were so, then every individual would be free to claim that their behaviour was acceptable. It appears as if the teachers are simply trying to ensure a reasonable standard of behaviour which conforms with the accepted norms of society. Relativism takes the view that there are no fixed or absolute standards in relation to knowledge about the world, moral behaviour, social organization, or any other aspect of human life. Extreme relativists would argue that each individual's view is just as valid as another person's view. The clear problem here is that the behaviour of some people is so extreme and unpleasant to society, that it is difficult to reconcile this with its being just another relativist form of human conduct.

On the other hand, attempts to fix absolute standards are not without difficulty. In the above example about schools, the standards of one school, while being fairly similar in broad respects, may not be identical to those of another school. In other words, the standards of each school are relative. There are some independent schools which have developed a rather different culture to that of mainstream state schools. Which culture is right? Is one better than another? These are the questions raised by the relativist debate.

see also...

Absolutism

Rights

Imagine that the government wishes to build a new motorway and that the best route for this will entail building on large areas of farmland. The government issues a notice saying that it will have to compulsorily purchase the land and the buildings on it. One farmer decides that he will not surrender his farm without a protracted legal struggle. When the government surveyor knocks at his door he says, 'You can't do this to me and my family; we have our rights.'

What is the farmer claiming under these circumstances? To start with he seems to be claiming what are often termed 'natural' rights. These are attributes and privileges which accrue to him by virtue of being a human. They include, presumably in this case, the right to live in his own home and not to be told to leave on the basis of a road planning decision of central government. This natural right is different from a 'legal' right. The farmer is claiming implicitly that it is unfair, unethical, unreasonable and essentially anti-human to try to evict him, simply because the government wishes to build its motorway in a particular position. It

is a claim, at least in part, that contrasts the rights of the individual with the rights of a centralized bureaucracy. In it may also be the implication that the farmer may not have voted for this government and, even if he did, he did not vote for it to evict him from his home.

Quite apart from the concept of natural rights, the farmer is also presumably alluding to his legal rights. He is asserting his rights to defend himself in the courts against the threat of eviction. He is perhaps claiming that simply because the government believes it is acting legally, that this may not in fact be the case. The issue should be tested in the courts. The concept of rights is often discussed in parallel with that of 'duties'. So, for example, while the state may reasonably have a right to build roads wherever it seems best for the common good, it also has a duty to protect the freedom of the individual to continue to live where he or she has always done.

see also...

Ethics

Ross, W.D.

Sir William Ross (1877–1971) was a British philosopher who, apart from his contributions to philosophy, was a noted translator of ancient Greek philosophical texts. He held a number of major academic posts including Provost of Oriel College, Oxford University and was also vice-chancellor of the same university. Ross worked mainly in the area of ethics, and did not subscribe to theories of ethics which judged the rightness or wrongness of actions either on the basis of the motives of the individual concerned or on the basis of the results of actions. Rather he proposed that some actions are intrinsically right and good, while some are wrong. Lying is thus wrong because it is fundamentally and intrinsically a wrong act. A person who lies, for example, may do so out of either wicked or noble motives. They may lie in order to defraud someone of money, or they may lie to a person who is seriously ill, telling them that their illness is not so serious after all, in order to save them stress and anxiety. In other words relying exclusively upon motives may not always tell us whether a particular generic type of action is ethically right or wrong. Similarly with the consequences of an action. Although lying may in particular circumstances appear to have favourable consequences, this does not necessarily make lying morally right.

Fundamentally, lying is wrong because we have a duty to other people to tell the truth. We are sensitive to this duty through a process of intuition. Similarly we are sensitive to a number of other basic moral duties. The appeal of this apparently straightforward analysis is that it is in agreement with much everyday moral teaching. Parents will often tell their children to always tell the truth, whatever the circumstances. Children will sometimes attempt to blur the ethics of truth-telling, adapting the principle to particular circumstances; yet parents will often make truth-telling an absolute virtue. The problem with such a theory, however, is how to reconcile moral duties based on a form of moral intuition.

see also...

Consequence Theories of Ethics;
Deontological Theories; Ethics

Scepticism

Some philosophers have expressed the view that it is very difficult to be certain of anything. In particular, they have argued that although empirical data may appear to generate knowledge and understanding, all it really does is to provide a series of sense impressions from the external world. These impressions, it is argued, are not the same as knowledge. Sceptics are people who doubt whether it is possible to know anything. There are sceptics who fall into different categories, ranging from those who literally feel it is not possible to know anything; to those people who feel that our capacity to know is extremely limited, but that we tend to act under normal circumstances as if we do believe certain things and have knowledge of them.

If we imagine looking at a chair, then our eyes receive light waves reflected from the wood which tell us that we are looking at a four-legged artefact with a back and flat piece of wood resting on the legs. That is the beginning and end of what the empirical data will tell us, or so some would argue. Our minds then carry out analytic work on that data and conclude that this object has much in common with other objects which have previously been classified as chairs and which have a particular function – that of being sat upon and supporting a human body. The mind has already conducted analytic work on objects classed as chairs, identifying their characteristics, and has identified the present object as possessing some of these features. There is still, though, no certainty in classing the new object as a chair. In the first case, sceptics might argue that the original analytic work performed on a range of 'chairs' may have been incorrect, and hence render the classification of the present object as inaccurate. In any case, sceptics could argue that there is not really an object which can be termed a 'chair'. The concept 'chair' is just a convenient construct for a certain general type of object upon which we sit. Perhaps, a sceptic could argue, it is just as well to define a chair in terms of what it does, rather than what it looks like.

see also...

Epistemology

Social Contract

A social contract is an implicit or explicit agreement between members of a society, expressing certain shared duties and obligations. The contract may be between a ruler and citizens, or between citizens themselves expressing a commitment to certain principles of government or societal organization. The social contract may be spoken of as if it is something which actually exists, whereas it is arguable whether individuals born into a particular society may be said to be party to any kind of contract. When children are born, they are reared within a particular societal and political framework, and are taught to adhere to the norms of that society. However, when they grow up, they may not necessarily subscribe to the particular ideology or value system of the society. A philosophical and particularly ethical question is whether an individual, who has gained many advantages from a society, is morally obliged to support that society. It may be, for example, that children who are able to attend good schools; who are cared for by a state health system; who are well fed and reared within a caring family structure, may grow into young adults who reject some aspects of the value system of that society.

The theory of the social contract arose from an imaginary situation where human beings were living in a natural condition without any form of government or organization. The assumption is that such an informal aggregation of people could be a hazardous environment in which to live, and under such circumstances people would be grateful to have a form of social organization. The next theoretical development is that people would elect or nominate a ruler with whom people in the new society would have a social contract. The ruler would protect them and organize the society, in exchange for allegiance and support from the citizens. This is the theoretical manner in which a social contract is seen as evolving. Yet the reality is much more complex, and it is at least an arguable position that the concept does not have a great deal of significance in contemporary society.

see also...

Democracy

Solipsism

Solipsism asserts that each human being has his or her own way of seeing the world, and that this constitutes reality for that person. If we wish to understand the ways in which we make sense of the world, then we must explore the nature of the consciousness of each individual human being.

The view that follows logically from this is that as human beings we are essentially isolated from each other, interpreting the world in our own unique fashion, and constructing our own subjective understandings of our surroundings. This could be interpreted as leading to a situation where individuals can have little real, meaningful communication, since each human being is operating from a different viewpoint. Some solipsists would also suggest that if the process of understanding the world is essentially cognitive in nature, there is little to be gained by studying the behaviour patterns and other external indicators of people. These are merely external manifestations of what is essentially an internal mental process of understanding the world.

From an epistemological perspective, solipsism leads us to the view that ultimately there are multiple, individual ways of knowing about the world, and indeed as many different epistemologies as there are people. If we accept that there are as many different conceptual frameworks as there are human beings, then this raises uncertainty about the possibility of meaningful dialogue between individuals.

From some perspectives solipsism is not a particularly optimistic viewpoint in terms of achieving consensus in, for example, the political arena. Even if one assumes it is possible for groups of people to achieve some agreement, particularly when linked by a particular political ideology, then there would appear to be less hope of such a group finding some measure of agreement with another ideologically oriented group. Solipsism, on one interpretation, appears to find compromise a difficult concept to envisage.

see also...

Relativism

89

Sophists

Sophists were individual travelling speakers and philosophers in ancient Greece. They travelled to religious festivals and other public events to give talks and conduct discussions. Sophists often charged for their services and gave instruction in public speaking and formulating arguments. It is difficult to identify a coherent set of views which one can attribute to the Sophists, although there are perhaps one or two identifiable themes. Perhaps the most famous Sophist was Protagoras who died in about 420 BCE. He argued famously that the individual human being was the yardstick by which knowledge should be judged. He considered that it was extremely difficult to know things with certainty, and hence individuals would have to make up their own minds on the evidence available. If there were any criteria to judge between different knowledge claims, then one should select the viewpoint which generally had the greatest practical utility. The Sophists were well known for teaching techniques to win arguments, rather than for the content of their teaching. They concentrated on what today might be termed social and communication skills.

In teaching the skills of argument, the Sophists probably laid the foundations of the study of linguistics. They were regarded as skilled educators and taught young people how to marshall arguments and to counteract the views of others. In Greek society, such skills were highly valued, and no doubt those who acquired these skills could use them to gain social mobility.

One difficulty with the Sophist teaching was that if one adopts a position as a subjectivist in terms of knowledge, it is difficult to know what one is teaching other than subjectivism. One can teach skills, but often skills are better understood and learned in relation to a particular theoretical basis, and this seems to have been largely lacking in the Sophists. If one wishes to teach scientific experimentation, it is often taught against a background of theoretical science.

see also...

Subjectivism

Stevenson, Charles

Charles Stevenson (1908–79) was an ethical theorist who taught at the University of Michigan. He was an advocate of what is commonly termed the Emotive Theory of ethics. Perhaps his most significant work was *Ethics and Language* (1944). Stevenson argued that when people make ethical judgements they are, in effect, articulating an emotive reaction to something, or giving expression to their feelings about it. For example, if someone says that violent videos should be completely banned, the emotive theory of ethics suggests that what is being said here is simply an expression of the feeling that violent videos are awful and nobody should be allowed to see them.

Implicit in this view is that moral statements such as this are significantly different from scientific statements. For example, one might hypothesize that the watching of violent videos has an adverse effect on the behaviour of teenagers. This would probably be a very difficult hypothesis to test, but at least we can recognize some provisional procedures which might be used to test the hypothesis. We can perhaps appreciate approximately the type of data needed. However, once we claim that such videos should be banned, we are making a moral claim, the veracity of which is apparently much harder to establish.

The problem with claiming that moral utterances are simply expressions of feelings is that this does not really accord with some of the moral thinking that goes on in society. The fact is, people do spend a lot of time debating moral issues and trying to decide whether action A or action B is preferable. When faced with an ethical problem many people devote a good deal of time to seeking an appropriate course of action. The emotive theory, so its critics would argue, reduces moral statements to a much too simplistic level, and ignores the sophistication of much ethical debate.

see also...

Ethics

Stoicism

This was a major school of philosophy in ancient Greece, which eventually became significant in Roman culture as well. It was founded by Zeno of Citium (*c.* 300 BCE) and other adherents included Chrysippus and Cleanthes. Perhaps the best known advocate of Stoic principles was the Roman emperor, Marcus Aurelius (121–180 CE). The early Stoics were probably influenced to some extent by the changing nature of society at the time, and their reaction was to be rather untrusting of the world. Stoics believed that the way to peace of mind was to be detached from the surrounding world. However, this did not necessarily mean withdrawing from the world. The general view of the Stoics was that it was reasonable to continue to live in the world, but that one should remain detached from both pleasure and pain. The latter two opposites were regarded as inevitable accompaniments to life in the world, yet Stoics argued that we should practise not being affected by them.

There are many parallels here with Hinduism and Buddhism. In the Hindu scripture, the Bhagavad Gita, part of the philosophical advice is that individuals should take part in worldly affairs, but should not become attached to the results of their actions. For example, if an attractive, well-paid job becomes vacant, then one should certainly apply for it, but having done so, one should forget about it. If one were to be continually thinking about the job and evaluating ones chances of success, then this would be likely to generate unhappiness. In Buddhism, also, there is a related concept of non-attachment. This stresses the importance of not becoming attached to the physical world. The advantage of this Stoic version of non-attachment is that it provides a sense of power for the individual. If, for example, a person is intimidated by a manager at work, it is often because the person is frightened of losing his or her job or of being demoted. The Stoic would argue that the individual is intimidated only because they are attached to the job and the financial security which it brings. Relinquishing that attachment brings a sense of freedom.

see also...

Asceticism

Subjectivism

Let us suppose that you hear someone say, 'It is a good thing to give to the poor.' A key question for moral philosophers is the meaning of such a pronouncement. If the intention is to suggest that there should be a general rule, then we perhaps might ask how much we ought to give to the poor and also how 'the poor' are to be defined. If, for example, someone is only slightly poorer than we are, should we then feel obliged to give? Equally well, we may not know who is poor in terms of their exact circumstances. We usually do not know the details of other people's assets and it may not be possible to know exactly, unless, for example, someone is clearly poverty-stricken. This raises the issue of whether we are considering absolute poverty, defined as being below a certain threshold annual income; or relative poverty, defined by comparing two sets of people with differential incomes. There is finally the question in this example, of whether one would want to give a small token amount of money, or a significant sum such as that required to rectify any imbalance between two sets of people.

The statement then, 'It is a good thing to give to the poor' raises a number of questions about conceptual precision. A subjectivist takes the view that it means approximately, 'I think that it is a good thing to give to the poor.' In other words, the speaker is acting as an advocate of this assertion, rather than necessarily trying to make it into a general law. To some extent it follows from this that disputes about ethical issues cannot really be resolved; or at least, that is the view of the subjectivist. The feeling here, is that since moral assertions are really only the equivalent of, 'I personally think this is a good thing', it is not really possible to evaluate competing claims.

Finally, since subjectivists claim that their personal views have validity, to some extent they are asserting that knowledge may reasonably be based upon individual views of the world. If, for example, I have found something to be true in the world, then I may legitimately claim it as true.

see also...

Objectivism

Sufficient Condition

These are the overall circumstances which must be present before an event can occur. For example, in order to be admitted to a theatre, it is normally a sufficient condition that one should have bought a ticket. Likewise, if a person wishes to be admitted to a cinema then the sufficient condition may be that he or she is both old enough for the particular classification of film, and has also purchased a ticket.

Some events are potentially very complex and require a wide range of conditions before they can take place. In the case of, say, an aeroplane taking off, there are clearly a great number of conditions. There should be fuel in the tanks; the engines must be functioning properly; there must be an acceptable weight of passengers and luggage, among many other factors. All of the pre-flight checks will take these into account. One way of looking at these conditions is to regard each individual condition as a necessary condition, and the sum total of the necessary conditions to be the sufficient condition. It is clearly a necessary condition for the aircraft to take off that there should be fuel in the tanks, but this alone is not sufficient. There are many other circumstances which must be in place.

Events in the physical world, such as engines and machinery working properly, are complex enough, but in the social world the sum total of the necessary conditions may be very extensive indeed, or perhaps even indefinable. For example, we might consider what the sufficient condition would be for a student at university to obtain a good degree. One might say that there is just one sufficient condition – that he or she must pass the final examinations with high marks. However, we could break down the progress of the student's studies into a number of sub-conditions. For example, the student should study regularly; attend lectures; follow the instructions of tutors; hand assignments in on time; read around the subject and so on.

see also...

Necessary Condition

Teleology

This is the study of the ultimate purposes of objects or living things; and also of the final ends of processes. One type of teleological question is whether we may regard a physical or biological process as simply being a process, or whether we see it as an activity directed towards a particular end. For example, once a combustive process has started, and assuming that the required temperature is maintained and oxygen is available, the assumption is that this chemical reaction is moving to an end when all of the combustive material has been used up. This kind of process may be seen as unidirectional and working towards a specific end. On the other hand, if we consider a biological process such as evolution, it is more difficult to envisage this as moving towards a specific end point. The fossil record suggests that there have, in the past, been many evolutionary trends which have ended with the extinction of organisms, while other more successful species have continued to exist. In other words it is very difficult to see evolution being directed towards a specific end. It perhaps seems more plausible to regard it as a continuing mechanism whereby organisms become adapted to a changing environment.

A number of major religions, particularly theistic religions, may be regarded as teleological in nature. There is often a concept of a divinity directing the overall purpose of the universe, and also having a particular view of the ultimate purpose of humanity – whether individually or collectively.

Teleology is concerned with the issue of ultimate purposes both on the micro, individual level, and also on the macro level of the universe. It is a genuinely metaphysical question, since notwithstanding the efforts of cosmologists and astronomers, it is difficult to establish the likely future of the universe. Within some cosmologies, for example that of the Hindu tradition, the universe is seen as passing through a series of cycles of almost infinite duration, rather than heading towards a single finite goal.

---

see also...

Ontology

Theory of Forms

This approach to the problems of the existence of knowledge derives from Plato and essentially argues that the fundamentals of knowledge already exist, and only require to be recognized by individual people. As an example, we can consider 'circular' objects which exist in nature. A pebble, the moon and the cross-section of a tree trunk may all be approximately circular. Although they are not exactly circular, we still retain within our minds the concept of a perfect circle. We may never expect to see one in natural circumstances, but we nevertheless understand the notion of perfect circularity.

The question posed by Plato is essentially how we come to understand the 'form' of circularity. Plato's answer to this problem is that the knowledge of a perfect circle is certainly not gained from observation or empirical understanding. We cannot gain it in this way because it simply does not exist. Hence, we must acquire the concept by recognizing that the knowledge of this is already within our minds. For Plato, the forms of knowledge are absolute, eternal and unchanging. They provide, among other things, a yardstick against which observations of individual examples can be measured.

The empirical world for Plato does not represent 'real' knowledge. The appearance of things is continually changing. The observed world is not truly dependable as a source of knowledge. The only way to come to true knowledge is to apply the principles of pure reason in order to understand the world of the forms. This is illustrated in one of Plato's Dialogues called *Meno*. Here Plato portrays Socrates discussing a geometrical problem with a slave boy. Socrates does not 'teach' the boy anything; but by a careful process of question and answer, leads the boy through a sequence of logical reasoning, resulting in the boy understanding the problem. The purpose of this is to suggest that the boy has an intrinsic understanding of the problem, but is not able to use this until he is helped to do so by Socrates.

see also...

Empiricism; Plato; Universals

Truth

I f a statement is regarded as true between people, then it must meet certain criteria or comply with certain standards. If we say that birds have wings, this is generally regarded as true. Some birds are indeed flightless, but they still have wings. In other words, we have no difficulty in identifying birds with wings, and this helps us in agreeing that the initial statement is probably true. This approach to truth is often known as the correspondence theory, since statements are considered true if they correspond to objects or events in the world. Sometimes, however, we are just not in a position to employ the correspondence theory. In response to someone who asserts that the earth is flat, we may say that it cannot be true because we have seen photographs of a round earth taken by astronauts in space. However, when the flat-earth believer retorts that such photographs are simply part of a large-scale confidence trick by the round-earth believers, and that the photographs were created in a studio, we may be left grasping for supporting evidence. Of course, we have not actually been into space ourselves and taken our own photographs, so it is a little difficult to point to a round earth in the same way we pointed to a winged bird.

Advocates of a round earth would probably at this point adduce a wide range of supporting evidence from cartographers, ship's captains, airline pilots and astronomers, to support the assertion that the world is in fact round. What they would be doing here would be to adopt what is often known as the coherence theory of truth. In other words, they would be seeking to establish that the concept of a round earth is an intrinsic part of a wider conceptual framework involving a range of academic disciplines, within which all of the constituent concepts of that framework operate as a coherent whole. All of the concepts essentially support each other, and it would be scarcely conceivable for a completely untrue concept to coexist within such a mutually supportive framework.

> ### see also...
> *Pragmatism*

Universals

A universal is the general property held by a number of objects or individuals, which each characterize that general property. For example, the universal 'movement', that property which entails being in the process of transferring from one place to another, may be exemplified by a number of individual examples. Birds flying, deer running, or fish swimming may all be cited as examples of that universal. Universals may also be abstract, as in the case of the universal 'goodness'. This may be reflected in particular examples, such as the self-sacrifice of one individual who tries to save another who is in peril; or the generosity of a person who gives money to assist another who is in great need.

One of the important philosophical questions about universals is whether they exist in some way independently of the particular instances, and hence that when we speak of them we merely uncover something which existed before. The alternative way of thinking about universals is that they are merely the creation of individual people to help them understand and categorize the world. Some philosophers (particularly those influenced by Plato) have held that universals have an independent existence, quite separate from the individual examples. Others have suggested, however, that a universal can only exist in parallel with the particular examples which characterize it. This view was propounded by the Greek philosopher Aristotle who was a student of Plato's at the Academy for two decades.

A further philosophical problem concerning universals is that of the mechanism by which they come into existence. On the one hand it would be possible to view them as the creation of the minds of human beings; while on the other, one could view them as existing independently of human minds. Linked to this question is the issue of whether universals can be said to exist at all.

see also...

Plato; Theory of Forms

98

Utilitarianism

This is an ethical theory which its advocates suggest can be used to evaluate the rightness or wrongness of an action. In forming ethical judgements, utilitarians argue that we should be primarily concerned with the consequences of actions. The best known way of expressing utilitarianism is that if we are comparing the ethical quality of two ways of acting, then we should choose the alternative which tends to produce the greatest happiness for the greatest number of people. Alternatively, we might want to select the action which generates the greatest pleasure or produces the most good.

As an example, if a violent civil war were to break out in a small remote country, the United Nations might consider sending in peace-keeping forces. However, the nations concerned would have to balance the good that intervention might achieve, with the risks to their own troops. There would need to be a weighing up of the moral pros and cons. This is exactly what utilitarians try to do in evaluating possible consequences. However, this leads us to one of the criticisms of utilitarianism, which is that it is not always possible to form a clear judgement about the consequences of an action and thereby know how to act. In the above kind of example, it is notoriously difficult to predict the long-term political consequences of intervention in foreign conflicts.

Utilitarianism is significant because it seeks to concentrate on the results of actions, rather than the motives of human beings when they are acting. For instance, two people may be driving cars in excess of the speed limit. One driver may be joy-riding, while the other may be rushing a sample of blood to a hospital for an emergency operation. The actions are the same, in terms of driving very fast, but the motives are entirely different. The issue of whether consequences are more important than motives is an interesting philosophical question. Utilitarianism is associated with the philosopher John Stuart Mill.

see also...

Consequence Theories of Ethics;
Ethics; Mill, John Stuart

Value

The value of an object or an idea is a measure of its inherent worth or the esteem in which it is publicly held. Value can be a quality which is attached to something by virtue of its intrinsic characteristics. For example, we might speak of the value of participative democracy, as referring to the qualities of a political system which provides for the close involvement of all sectors of society. The term participative democracy implies an essential quality of involvement, and therein lies its value.

We may also argue that such inherent value is also to be found in a work of art, such as a renaissance painting. The question arises, however, whether the essential worth of the painting is somehow a permanent feature of it and can be distinguished by different people, or whether its value is simply a matter of artistic taste. In the former case, the question is raised as to whether one needs a special sort of perception or even training to distinguish the value of art. If the value is there as a permanent feature of the painting, we perhaps need to explain why not all people can

recognize this. On the other hand, if value is simply a matter of personal taste, then it is difficult to see that the painting has some essential quality which we can hold up as worthy of the term 'value'. This discussion raises the question of whether value should be seen as either a subjective or objective quality.

Some qualities or activities may be seen as having both intrinsic value and also having value in terms of practical utility. One might argue, for instance, that education has intrinsic value. It seems reasonable to assert that acquiring a greater knowledge and understanding of the world is a good thing in itself. To participate in education is simply a valuable activity. However, having an education can also be useful in practical terms. If we think of education as both an end and a process, then to 'become educated', as an end, can be useful in terms of getting a better job and earning more money. We can say, therefore, that education has instrumental value.

see also...

Ethics; Pragmatism

Voluntarism

This is a general philosophical position which emphasizes the importance of individual choice in a range of spheres of human activity. An important issue for voluntarism as a principle, is whether it is being argued that the human will *is* an important factor in selecting a belief or an ethical principle, or whether it *should* be an important factor. Voluntarism, in general terms, emphasizes the role of the individual human will.

In ethical decisions, for example, voluntarists would argue that the decision which is eventually arrived at may derive, to some extent, from an understanding of generally accepted ethical principles, but may at the end of the day, depend more upon the simple action of the individual will. In other words this would be a decision of the order, 'I prefer, on balance, this line of action, to that line of action.' For example, someone may observe a fight underway outside a club and wonder whether to intervene, or indeed what action to take. All sorts of possible actions come to mind, such as telephoning the police, trying to enlist the help of passers-by to stop the fight; walking up to those involved and appealing quietly to their better nature; or simply walking away. There may be philosophical arguments in favour of, and against, each line of action, but ultimately a voluntarist would argue that the decision will depend upon individual choice.

Voluntarism may also be applied to such macro contexts as the course of history and to the place of individual human beings in large organizations. Voluntarists would argue that the course of history, for example, is not conditioned by any necessary evolutionary plan and set of predetermined social and economic forces, but largely depends upon individual human beings choosing to act in certain ways. Clearly, relatively few people have been in a position to influence the course of history to any great extent, but voluntarists would argue that the decisions they have chosen to make have had a greater influence overall than any larger historical forces.

see also...

Free Will

Further Reading

Almond, B. (ed.) (1995) *Introducing Applied Ethics*. Oxford: Blackwell.

De Beauvoir, S. (1972) *The Second Sex*. Harmondsworth: Penguin.

Ennis, R.H. (1996) *Critical Thinking*. New Jersey: Prentice Hall.

Flew, A. (1971) *An Introduction to Western Philosophy*. London: Thames and Hudson.

Gaarder, J. (1996) *Sophie's World*. London: Phoenix.

Habermas, J. (1978) *Knowledge and Human Interests*. London: Heinemann.

Harre, R. (1983) *An Introduction to the logic of the sciences*. London: Macmillan.

Hughes, J. (1997) *The Philosophy of Social Research*. New York: Longman.

Kuhn, T.S. (1970) *The Structure of Scientific Revolutions*. Chicago: Chicago University Press.

Magee, B. (1973) *Popper*, London: Collins.

Magee, B. (1988) *The Great Philosophers*. Oxford: Oxford University Press.

McGinn, C. (1992) *Moral Literacy, or How to do the right thing*. London: Duckworth.

Pinchin, C. (1990) *Issues in Philosophy*. London: Macmillan.

Popper, K.R. (1968) *The Logic of Scientific Discovery*. London: Hutchinson.

Popper, K.R. (1972) *Conjectures and Refutations*. London: Routledge.

Pratt, V. (1978) *The Philosophy of the Social Sciences*. London: Methuen.

Searle, J.R. (1996) *The Construction of Social Reality*. London: Penguin.

Singer, P. (1983) *Hegel*. Oxford: Oxford University Press.

Solomon, R.C. (1997) *Introducing Philosophy*. Fort Worth: Harcourt Brace.

Solomon, R.C. and Higgins, K.M. (1997) *A Passion for Wisdom*. Oxford: Oxford University Press.

Taylor, C. (1985) *Philosophy and the Human Sciences*. Cambridge: Cambridge University Press.

Thompson, M. (1994) *Ethics*. London: Hodder Headline.

Thompson, M. (1995) *Philosophy*. London: Hodder Headline.

Thomson, A. (1996) *Critical Reasoning*. London: Routledge.

Please note that classical works and editions mentioned in the text are often available through an academic library.

Also available in the series